DATE DUE

JAN 2 6 1995	SEP 1 6 1996
APR 0 5 1995	
AUG 2 1995	FEB 2 8 1997
AUG 2 3 1995	SEP 9 1997
JUN 1 5 1996	
	DEC 0 1 1999
DEC 3 1996	
APR 2 3 1997	Dec 15 1999
NOV 0 2 1997	
APR 0 9 2000	

GAYLORD   PRINTED IN U.S.A.

The Kalstone Guide to
GROOMING ALL TOY DOGS

by Shirlee A. Kalstone

Photographs by Larry Kalstone
Drawings by Vivian Falzetti

First Edition

HOWELL BOOK HOUSE
New York

Howell Book House
Macmillan Publishing Company
866 Third Avenue, New York, NY 10022

Collier Macmillan Canada, Inc.
1200 Eglinton Avenue East, Suite 200
Don Mills, Ontario M3C 3N1

Library of Congress Catalog Card No. 75-25248

ISBN 0-87605-323-1

Macmillan books are available at special discounts for bulk purchases for sales promotions, premiums, fund-raising, or educational use. For details, contact:

Special Sales Director
Macmillan Publishing Company
866 Third Avenue
New York, NY 10022

10 9 8

Printed in the United States of America

Contents

Acknowledgements

I wish to express my gratitude to the following for their interest and assistance:

Frank Oberstar, Richard Ball, Gini Evans—Past President of the American Maltese Association, Barbara Stubbs of the Chaminade Kennels, Jo Ann White (professional handler and owner of the Heavenly Dynasty Shih Tzu Kennels), Velma and Jim Rees (owners of Ch. Gin-Doc's Hiawatha of Lou-J, the Shih Tzu used to illustrate coat wrapping), Mrs. Gemma Nachtigal, Mrs. Racille Karelitz, Susan Mechem and Mrs. Walter Kaufman. Lastly, a special "Thank You" to the pet owners who let us photograph their matted dogs.

Some of the dogs whose photographs illustrate their breed chapters are considered outstanding specimens of their respective kinds. We thank their owners for the use of their reproductions in this book.

Affenpinscher	Ch. Walhof Teddy Bear
Bichons Frises	Dogs of the Chaminade Kennels
Brussels Griffons	Stouravon Gerrard's Jack in a Box (Smooth)
	Ch. Barmere's Marianne (Rough)
	Ch. Arsenal Tout Suite of Kildare (Rough, head study)
Cavalier King Charles Spaniel	English Ch. Requiem of Ottermouth
Chihuahua	Ch. Weeville's Tis So Too (Smooth)
Chinese Crested Dog	Yan Cee
English Toy Spaniel	Ch. Zepherine Lysander
Italian Greyhound	Ch. Queen's Alfa vom Bayerischen Meer
Japanese Spaniel	English Ch. Gorsdene Hirohito of Yevot
Lhasa Apso	Ch. Chen Korum Ti
Maltese	Ch. Aennchen's Poona Dancer
Miniature Pinscher	Ch. Rebel Roc's Casanova v. Kurt
Papillon	English Ch. Stouravon Young Tammy
Pekingese	Ch. Wei Tiko of Pekeboro
Pomeranian	Ch. Rider's Sparklin' Gold Nugget
Toy Poodle	Ch. Fieldstream's Bojangles
Pug	Ch. Pugholm's Peter Punkin Eater
Silky Terrier	Ch. Lylac Blue Prince (headstudy)
Tibetan Terrier	Ch. Miss Tuppence of Kathmandu and Tehdeh Phurba of Shahi-Taj
Toy Manchester Terrier	Ch. Golden Scoop's Lady Rowena
Yorkshire Terrier	Ch. Murose Exquisite and Ch. Murose Sweet Pippa

Introduction

This book was written because there has been a shortage of written material on grooming Toy dogs. While it deals mainly with instructions for the Toy breeds, three breeds from the Non-Sporting Group (Bichon Frise, Lhasa Apso and Tibetan Terrier) are included because of similarities in coat care and finishing techniques.

The first half of the book includes information on basic care for all the breeds. The beginning chapters, *Choosing The Correct Grooming Equipment* and *Grooming Tips For Beginners*, will give you a good grooming foundation and the necessary general information to help control your dog. The second half of the book contains detailed grooming instructions for the various breeds.

Before you attempt any grooming, read all of the chapters in the first half of the book and learn the correct way to brush, comb, bathe and dry your dog, plus other important information on care of the eyes, ears and nails and how to control parasites. Then turn to the grooming instructions for your particular breed.

Instructions are included for pet and show grooming of the various breeds. Many of these dogs are long coated and do not require extensive clipping or scissoring, but do need regular coat care on a daily basis to maintain the appearance which best conforms to their breed standard.

Whether you see this book to care for your dog between professional appointments or to do all the grooming yourself, remember that nothing will help you to become an expert more than practice. Each day, try to set aside some time to work on your dog. Your grooming techniques will improve and your dog will associate grooming time as a pleasant experience.

Photograph 1. The Oster Model A5 Small Animal Clipper.

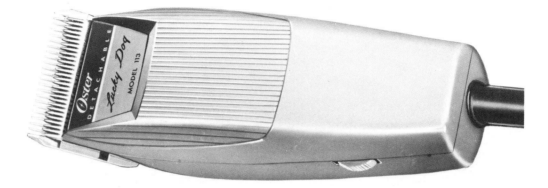

Photograph 2. The Oster Model 113 Lucky Dog Clipper.

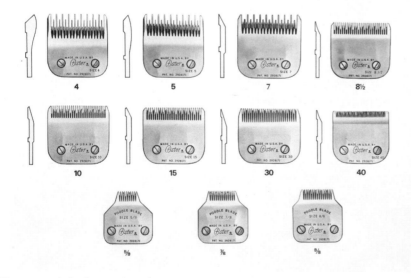

Photograph 3. Oster electric clipper heads are available to meet any clipping need.

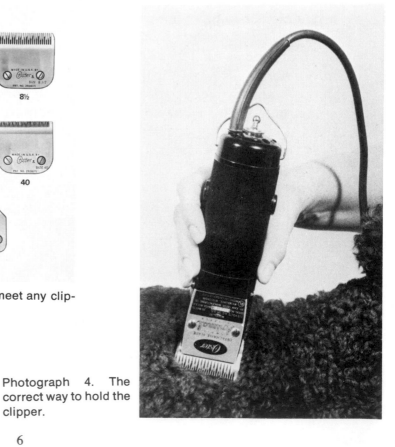

Photograph 4. The correct way to hold the clipper.

Choosing the Correct Grooming Equipment

Once you decide to learn how to groom your dog, the next consideration is the selection of the correct grooming equipment to do a thorough job. Listed below and clearly defined for easy selection, are the various tools mentioned in the grooming instructions which follow. Be sure to study the basic and specific breed grooming instructions to determine which tools are necessary. Most beginners tend to overbuy equipment and, without guidance, often select the wrong tools. One word of advice, regardless of whether you are interested in pet, show or professional grooming, always purchase quality equipment for the best always costs less in the long run.

Clippers and Blades

Because different blades can be used to clip a dog's hair to various lengths, it is best to purchase a clipper with changeable blades. Most professionals prefer Oster Clippers because they are durable and perform smoothly. There are several Oster models with a variety of detachable blades that can be changed quickly and easily. For professional or show grooming, the Oster Model A-5 Clipper is the most advanced model with 10 detachable blades. For home grooming, the Oster Model 113 is inexpensive, small and lightweight, and has 5 detachable blades. The various blades are listed below. The numbered blades are for the A-5 model. Corresponding blades for the Model 113 are listed in parentheses:

#4—leaves the hair about 3/4″ long.

#5 (Skip Tooth)—leaves the hair about 1/2″ long.

#7 (Coarse)—leaves the hair about 1/4″ long.

#8-1/2—leaves the hair about 1/8″ long.

#10 (Medium)—shows the natural color of the coat. Good for animals with sensitive skins and for use on stomach area.

#15 (Fine)—clips closer than #10.

#30—close cutting. Recommended for Poodle clipping only.

#5/8 (#5/8—also available for Model 113)—blade is 5/8″ wide. Recommended for hard-to-get spots.

#7/8—blade is 7/8″ wide.

#8/8—blade is 1″ wide.

REMEMBER: A blade cuts closer when used against the growth of hair than when used with the growth. Thus #10 blade used against the growth of hair (from the tail to the head) equals the same look as a #15 blade used with the growth (from the head to the tail). Similarly, a #15 blade used against the growth looks the same as a #30 used with the growth.

Always keep your clippers oiled and lubricated. Do not be alarmed if your new clipper seems sluggish when you begin clipping. Use the clipper for several weeks and it will work up to maximum performance.

At the end of each clipping session, clean all the blades you used in the following manner with Oster Blade Kleen, a cleaner and lubricant made especially for Oster Clipper blades:

A. Remove all hairs that have clogged in the blade's teeth with the clipper brush.
B. Pour a small amount of Blade Kleen into a shallow container and drop blades in the solution.
C. After soaking a few minutes, remove blades from solution and wipe dry with a clean cloth.

Occasionally, during the clipping operation, you can submerge the cutting blades in Blade Kleen while the clipper is running. This cleans and lubricates the blades and helps to improve the clipper's performance. Clean blades will not need sharpening as often as neglected ones. Never use the same blade on more than one dog without disinfecting it after each use. Parasites and skin diseases are spread through neglecting to do this. Most professionals use a spray lube to keep their clipper blades in good condition during the grooming process. These products are sprayed directly onto the blade. In addition to improving performance, the spray lube cools, sterilizes and keeps hair from accumulating in the blade. In between use, clipper blades should be oiled, wrapped in the brown paper in which they were originally packed and stored in a dry place to prevent rusting.

The best position for holding the clippers is shown in Photograph 4. The clipper is held almost as you would hold a pencil. When in use, always place the blade flat against the area you are clipping. Never point the front edge of the blade into the skin as this may cause scratching and clipper burn.

Scissors

Whichever type of scissor is necessary for your breed, always buy the finest model you can afford. Fine quality scissors hold an edge longer than inexpensive scissors. Scissors of poor quality will always need to be sharpened more often than expensive models, you will not save money in the long run. The various types of scissors recommended in the grooming instructions are:

BARBER SCISSORS: with long, straight blades tapering to a point. Mostly used for finishing work and all-over scissoring, barber scissors are purchased by length. A 7″ scissor is recommended as a comfortable size for Toy Breeds and a 7-1/2″ or 8″ scissor suggested for the medium-sized breeds.

BLUNT-EDGE SCISSORS: with curved blades and rounded tips. Best choice for scissoring a fidgety dog.

NASAL SCISSORS: with short, straight blades and a rounded ball tip. Overall length is from 4″ to 5″. Recommended for all Toy breeds, especially those with short hair, for scissoring facial whiskers and in between the toes, etc.

Photographs 9 and 10 show the correct position for holding the scissors. Slip your

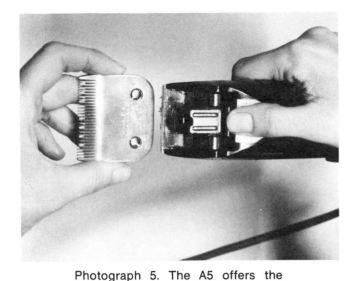

Photograph 5. The A5 offers the groomer the convenience of being able to change the blade by merely snapping off one and snapping in another.

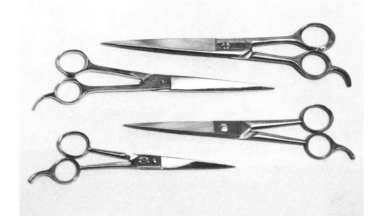

Photograph 6. In any grooming operation, good barbers' shears are imperative. Buying less than the best is a false economy.

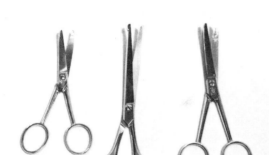

Photograph 7. Blunt-edged scissors are recommended particularly for working with nervous dogs or with puppies.

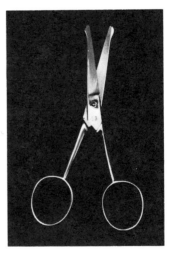

Photograph 8. The small size and overall design of the nasal scissor make it ideal for trimming facial whiskers and other fine trimming operations on all Toy breeds.

Photograph 9. In the photo above and in the one to the right is demonstrated two ways to correctly handle the shears. You should always use the position most comfortable for you and that gives you the best trimming results.

Photograph 10.

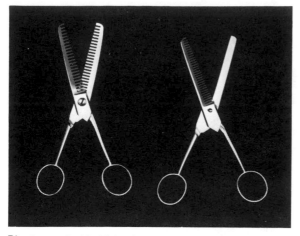

Photograph 11. Thinning shears are available in either single serrated or double serrated types.

Photograph 12. The slicker brush is an excellent tool in almost all pet grooming situations. For most show grooming operations, however, its use is discouraged.

Photograph 13. The pin brush is the brush of choice for most of the show grooming in Poodles and breeds with long, flowing coats. Several sizes are readily available.

Photograph 14. The bristle brush may be used with good result for all medium-coated and long-coated pets and show dogs.

Photograph 15. The palm brush is useful with some medium-coated dogs and all short-haired types. The hand strap enhances general ease of grooming.

thumb through the larger of the two openings. Then put your second or third finger (try both to determine which is most comfortable for you) through the smaller opening.

Thinning Shears

Single- or double-edged thinning shears may be purchased with 22, 24, 30 or extra-fine (46) teeth. Single-edged thinning shears have one regular scissor blade and one serrated blade. Double-edged thinning shears have both blades serrated. Most professionals prefer the 30-or 46-tooth single-edge shears because the finer serrations give smoother results. Thinning shears do not cut like barber scissors but rather, as their name implies, are used when long feathering or thick hair is to be thinned or blended into shorter hair.

Thinning shears are held in the same position as regular scissors. When in use, for best results, hold the shears vertically or with the growth of the coat, close to the skin. Never thin the tips of the hair or hold the shears horizontally or across the coat, as this will leave noticeable ridges in the dog's hair.

Brushes

The various types of brushes recommended in the grooming chapters are:

SLICKER BRUSH: an oblong-shaped brush with wooden handle. The slicker has bent wire teeth set close together to help remove mats and dead hair from pets. Slicker brushes are available in 3 sizes—small, for toy breeds; medium for medium-sized breeds and large for heavily coated or large dogs.

PIN BRUSH: recommended for long-coated breeds, especially dogs with long, flowing coats and all long-haired show dogs. Pin brushes have long, polished pins with rounded ends to prevent scratching and skin irritation. The long pins are set in a backed rubber cushion. When passing through the long coat, the pins are pliable enough not to pull out hair. The best pin brushes have pins made of solid brass or stainless steel. Brass pins help to reduce the amount of static electricity when the hair is brushed. Pin brushes are available in various sizes for small, medium and large breeds.

BRISTLE BRUSHES: recommended for medium and long-coated breeds, including show dogs. Made of either natural or nylon bristles, the finest brushes are made with bristle tufts set in a rubber cushion. The bristles in each tuft should be graduated in length to assure even and deep penetration through the coat to the skin. Available in all bristle or pure bristle with a surrounding core of lightweight nylon.

PALM BRUSH: oval bristle brush with leather handstrap for brushing ease. Palm brushes are available in a variety of bristle types: soft, for sensitive-skinned pets; medium, the best choice for the average short-haired dog to prevent scratching and skin irritation and firm, for maximum penetration on medium-coated pets.

RUBBER BRUSH: flexible, rubber bristles which polish the coat and help remove dead hair from short-haired breeds without scratching. This brush also makes an excellent shampoo brush.

Combs

Dog combs come in many different styles and a variety of widths. Select a fine-tooth comb for soft, sparse or silky hair; a medium-tooth comb for average texture,

Photograph 16. The rubber brush is ideal for polishing the coats of short-haired dogs and also doubles as an excellent shampoo brush.

Photograph 17. The terrier pad is essential for grooming harsh-coated dogs. No brush can do a better job on the body coat and furnishings of a Brussels Griffon for example.

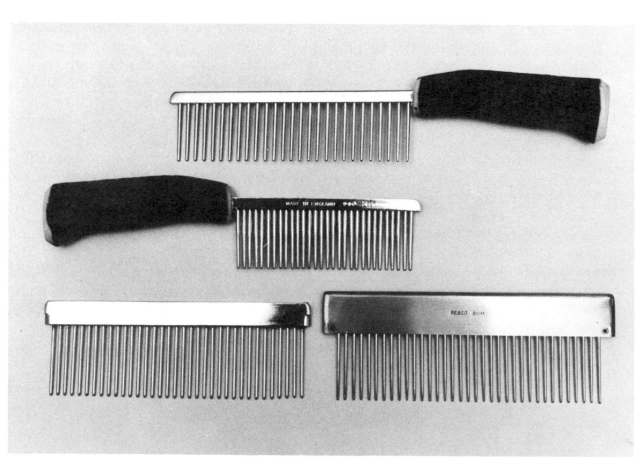

Photograph 18. The rake comb is recommended for the very heavy-coated breeds.

Photograph 19. The half fine—half medium combination comb is an excellent, all-purpose comb and the favorite grooming tool of many. It is made in different sizes to fit any longhaired breed.

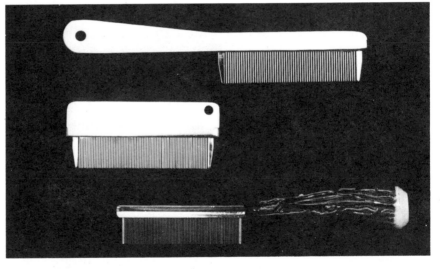

Photograph 20. The flea comb is a very fine-toothed tool and finds more use in combing face furnishings on long-haired Toys today than it does in dealing with parasites. Like most other dog combs, the flea comb can be had with or without a handle. Some groomers prefer dog combs without them.

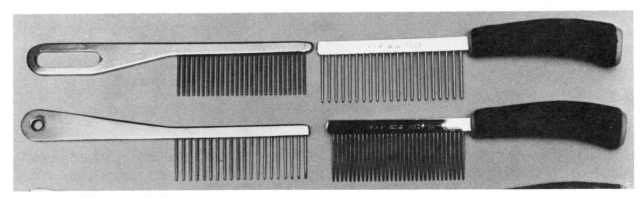

Photograph 21. Combs with handles are made in many types and styles for all types of grooming operations. They are particularly useful with medium or long coats.

and a coarse-tooth comb for dense or thick-textured hair. Always buy the finest comb you can afford. The best models are made of chrome-plated brass and have spring-tempered teeth with rounded tips to prevent scratching and skin irritation. The various types of combs recommended in the grooming chapters are:

RAKE COMB: recommended for use on coarse-textured or large breeds. The long medium-spaced teeth make this an excellent choice for the heavy-coated Lhasa Apso or Tibetan Terrier.

HALF-FINE, HALF-MEDIUM COMBINATION COMB: available in several sizes and styles, this is the best ''all purpose'' comb for long-haired toy breeds, especially the long, flowing-coated breeds like the Maltese, Shih Tzu, Yorkshire Terrier, etc.

COMBS WITH HANDLES: Recommended for medium and long-coated toy dogs. Available in various widths with teeth about 1″ long.

FLEA COMBS: Available with or without handle. The style with handle also doubles as an extra-fine tooth facial comb to remove matter or dirt caked in the facial hair near the eyes.

Stripping Comb

A stripping comb is a tool with a steel blade and wooden handle. The blade has one edge serrated in fine, medium or coarse widths. For the toy breeds requiring stripping, a fine- and medium-tooth stripping comb is necessary. The medium stripping comb is used for body and leg work, while the fine comb is used for the head area.

The correct position for holding the stripping comb is shown in Photograph 22. Hold the front of the comb handle in the palm of your hand, curling your fingers around the back of the handle, and rest your thumb on the blade.

Nail Clippers

The most popular type of nail clipper is the guillotine model shown in the photograph. The nail is inserted in the opening. When the handles are squeezed together, a blade passes over the opening, cutting off a portion of the dog's nail, hence the name ''guillotine'' model.

Hemostat

Cleaning the ears of any long-haired breed is an important part of grooming. For the toy and medium-sized breeds, a straight 5″ Kelly Forceps is best for removing excess hair from the ears.

Hair Dryer

Many of the small, long-haired breeds must be brushed dry after bathing to make the coat hang correctly. The Oster Company manufactures an inexpensive model dryer for home grooming called the Airjet. This dryer can be purchased at most pet or department stores and attachments are available to convert it to a human dryer.

For professional or show grooming, heavy duty dryers which dry a long coat in a few minutes are available from Edemco, Oster, Petlift and Safari.

Grooming Table

Selection of a grooming table is important. It must be sturdy, not wobbly or shaky.

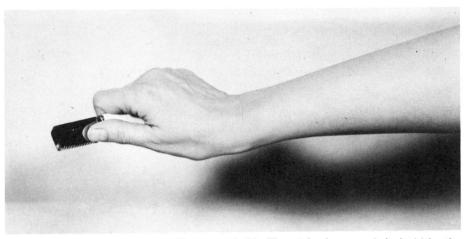

Photograph 22. The stripping comb is held in the hand with four fingers curling around the handle. The thumb rests against the blade and the coat is pulled only in the direction it grows.

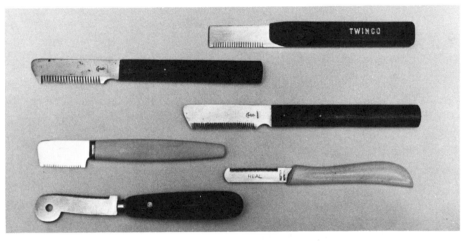

Photograph 23. Stripping combs are made in many sizes and styles. The choice of which to buy depends on the breed and the body area to be stripped. As an example; you would not use the same tool on a Griffon's back as you would its ears.

Photograph 24. Clipping nails is essential to good dog grooming, and the most popular tool for this is the guillotine type.

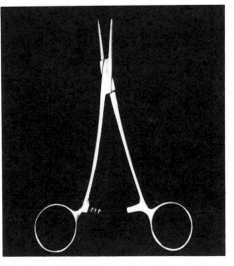

Photograph 25. Many long-haired dogs will grow hair in the ear canal. This should be regularly plucked out and the instrument of choice for Toys is the 5″ Kelly forceps.

Photograph 26. Electric hair dryers not only speed drying time but also help to achieve a more finished look to the final grooming of long-haired dogs. This model can be used on a grooming table or mounted on a cage front.

For the professional groomer or kennel owner, cage-drying smooth and certain medium-coated breeds saves a lot of valuable time.

Place a large, dry towel inside a cage. Remove the dog from the tub, towel the excess moisture from the coat and place the dog inside the cage. Attach the cage dryer, turn on the heat and let the hot air dry the dog, leaving you free to do other grooming. There are several precautions to observe with this method of drying:

1. Check the dog often—wet animals sometimes try to get as close as possible to the heat. If your cage is metal, be sure the dog is not leaning on the part of the cage where the dryer is attached. This could possibly burn the skin.

2. Be sure the air circulates freely through the top and sides of the cage. If the cage is all metal, do not cover the top and sides with towels in an effort to make the dog dry faster or the dog may possibly suffocate.

This method is not recommended for breeds that are fluffed dried (Bichon Frise, Poodle) or breeds with long, flowing coats (Maltese, Shih Tzu, etc.) that must be brushed dry to make the air hang straight.

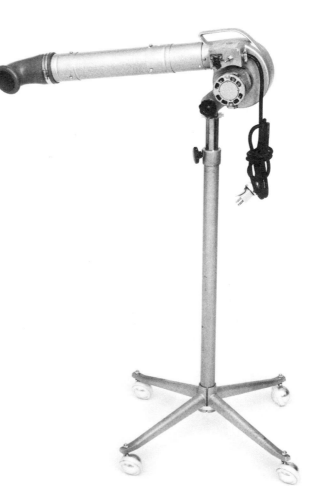

Photograph 27. This hair dryer is a heavy-duty floor model. It is usually found in grooming shops and professional kennels. It can dry the heaviest coats in a very short time.

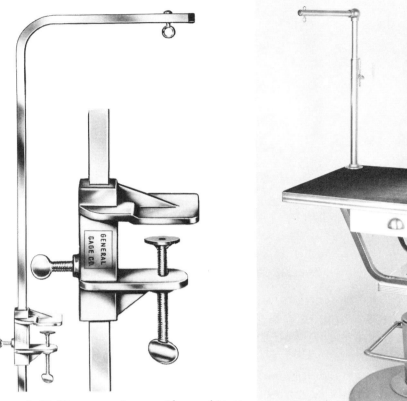

Photograph 28. The grooming post is used to restrain and quiet the dog on the table. The model shown here can be used with any grooming table.

Photograph 29. No experienced groomer would consider working on a dog without using a proper table. A good grooming table must be a comfortable height, sturdy and be equipped with a non-skid surface. The model illustrated here is of a very advanced design and features a height adjustment pedal, a revolving top and a storage drawer.

Many firms make inexpensive professional tables, 24″ x 36″, covered with a non-slip rubber top. These tables fold up and can be stored away when not in use. Many professional groomers and handlers use adjustable tables with a hydraulic foot pedal to raise or lower the dog to personal comfort. If you do not wish to buy a professional table, use any rigid table that is comfortable to work on. One that is about 30″ high, or half-way between your hip and knee will be less tiring. If the table has a smooth top, buy some grooved rubber matting at any hardware store to put on the table top to keep the dog from slipping. Small dogs can be groomed by placing a rubber mat on top of an automatic dryer until you locate a suitable table.

Grooming Post

A tubular post which is designed to be attached to a grooming table. At the end of the post is a loop which slips around the dog's neck to keep him from moving about or jumping off the table.

Grooming Tips for Beginners

1. If you are a beginner, do not attempt any grooming until you have read the trimming instructions for the breeds you are interested in.

2. Always use the proper equipment. The grooming instructions for each breed tell what tools are used for trimming. Then study the Equipment Chapter and learn about these grooming tools, what job each one does and how to use it properly. Most beginners tend to overbuy equipment, so before you purchase haphazardly, select the proper tools for the breeds you want to do.

3. Good grooming behavior should be taught at an early age—and can be—if you remember two basic rules:
   (A) Dogs learn by repetition, correction and praise.
   (B) Dogs should associate grooming with a pleasant experience.

4. Use a firm table for grooming. Since dogs learn by repetition, each time you brush or groom your dog, put him on this table. Eventually, your dog will learn that he must behave when he is being groomed. Never use an unsteady table—the dog will be frightened and try to jump off.

5. Make sure your grooming table has a non-slip rubber top. For your own comfort, so that you won't have to bend down so often to groom a small dog or stand on tip-toe to groom a large breed, invest in an adjustable grooming table.

6. Do your grooming in a room with adequate lighting. Have light coming from above and behind you. This is especially important when working on dark colored dogs or breeds with prominent eyes like the Pekingese, Shih Tzu, etc.

7. Don't expect your dog to stay perfectly still for hours on the grooming table when you first begin grooming. Dogs must be trained to behave on the table. Young puppies have short periods of concentration and will not stand still very long. If your puppy is very young, plan no more than fifteen to twenty minutes of grooming at one time. A good way to begin table training is to stand the puppy on the table for brushing. Place your free hand under the stomach for support (and to give the puppy confidence), then quickly run a brush through the coat. Speak quietly and reassuringly to the dog. At first, he may squirm about but, if you repeat this procedure every day for about two weeks, he will learn to stay still and behave.

8. If your dog will be shown in the breed ring, teach him to lie on his side while he

is being brushed. It takes a great deal of time to brush out a long-coated show dog. If the dog learns to lie on his side, he can rest while being brushed and you will find it easier to brush out the hair on the chest and the insides of his legs.

9. If your dog is frightened by the sound of the clippers, hold him in your lap and rest the clippers near his back with the motor running. He will become accustomed to the noise.

10. When grooming, you must learn to be firm without being mean. Never slap your dog to make him behave on the grooming table. If he disobeys, correct him until he does what you want, then *praise him!* When correcting the dog, use a firm tone of voice and pick one word for correction, such as *"Stop"* or *"No,"* but make sure you always use the same word so that your dog understands what you want him to do. Do be consistent. Don't let your dog get away with something one day, then reprimand him for doing the same thing the next day.

11. Toy dogs are very sensitive to the tones of the human voice. If you lose your patience, immediately stop whatever you are doing and take the dog off the table. Remember, the dog must not think of grooming as an unpleasant experience, so postpone the session until another time if you think you are losing control.

12. Do not talk baby talk to the dog or play with him while he is on the grooming table. He is there to be groomed, not to play games. Reward him with a biscuit or treat when the grooming session is finished if he has been cooperative.

13. Do not use clippers or scissors on a dirty dog. This dulls equipment quickly.

14. Scissors must be sharp and loose. Tight scissors prevent smooth scissoring. Check the photographs in the Equipment Chapter for the correct positions for holding barber and thinning scissors.

15. When scissoring near the vulva or testicles, place your free hand over them for protection. There is no excuse for nicking a dog's genitals. He will never forget it and will not cooperate the next time he is groomed.

16. Many toy breeds have large, protruding eyes set in shallow sockets which can be easily irritated by improper grooming. Refer to the Brushing, Bathing and Eye Care Chapters before you first groom any of these breeds.

17. Never cut out mats from the coat. If your dog is matted, follow suggestions found in the Brushing and Coat Problems Chapters.

18. Never give a toy dog a tranquilizer or anything that contains a harmful drug without a veterinarian's advice. Toy dogs can be dangerously allergic to drugs.

19. Follow this sequence each time you groom your dog:

    (A) Thoroughly brush and comb the dog to remove tangles and/or dead hair.
    (B) Clip toenails and clean ears.
    (C) Check anal glands.
    (D) Check skin for parasites.
    (E) Do any clipping or stripping work in the rough, if necessary.
    (F) Bathe and dry the dog. Apply Creme Rinse, Tangle Remover or parasite treatment if necessary.
    (G) Do final clipping or stripping work.
    (H) Do any body and leg scissoring or thinning.
    (I) Finish head area last. Groom topknot, brush facial hair or tie up forelocks as per grooming instructions for individual breed.

20. If you are a professional groomer, always keep a reliable rectal thermometer on hand. Being able to recognize a high temperature or serious illness quickly is

important for a toy dog. A dog's normal temperature is 101.5°. In puppies and adult Italian Greyhounds, Chihuahuas and Chinese Crested Dogs, it runs slightly higher. To take the temperature correctly, shake the thermometer down to below 94°. Grease the tip with vaseline and gently insert it into the dog's rectum, so that the bulb is completely covered. Hold the thermometer in place for a few minutes, then gently remove.

Recommendation: A copy of ALL ABOUT TOY DOGS *by Viva Leone Ricketts (Howell Book House) is a must for all toy dog owners or professional groomers. The chapters on Infectious Diseases, Home Nursing, Symptoms Of Illness, First Aid, Common Ailments and Accidental Poisoning are invaluable. When a small dog needs medical attention, there is a crucial span of time when what one does or does not do spells out the difference between success or failure.*

Brushing the Hair

Introduction

Brushing your dog's hair several times a week is the best way to keep the coat in good condition. On short-haired breeds, regular brushing keeps the skin clean and makes the dog less susceptible to skin disease and parasites. On long-haired breeds, brushing removes the dead hair before it has a chance to mat and stimulates the growth of new hair. A well-brushed coat is naturally oily and grows faster. The individual hairs lie more smoothly and the natural oil is distributed more evenly. A certain light is reflected from well-brushed hair and it looks more glossy than unbrushed hair.

Selection and use of the correct brush plays an important part in the health of your dog's skin and coat. Using the wrong brush or the wrong technique for brushing the hair can break off the ends or damage the coat.

Good brushing behavior should begin at an early age. As soon as you acquire your puppy, get it accustomed to being placed on a steady grooming table. While the puppy is young, place your hand under the stomach for support and confidence as you gently brush through the coat. Doing this several times a week is all that is necessary to make the dog behave and think of brushing as a pleasant experience. In the case of a long-haired dog, as the coat grows longer, the dog will become accustomed to behaving on the table while being brushed.

A thorough brushing is a prerequisite for a perfect grooming job on any breed. Because many small dogs spend much of their time inside the house, the combination of heat and a dry atmosphere often results in coat problems. To prevent dryness and keep the coat lustrous, before brushing, spray the hair with an aerosol conditioner. There are many excellent light oil coat conditioners—Ring 5 Protein Conditioner, Lambert Kay's Pro Groom, St. Aubrey Wonder Coat and many others, all available at pet or grooming shops everywhere. The aerosol conditioners which contain protein are a good choice for the pet owner. They are less greasy than most products and do not create a fast oil build-up on the coat.

Brushing Short-Haired Breeds

Short-haired breeds require a minimum of time-consuming brushing. The most important factor comes from within on a short-haired dog. Feeding the dog properly, supplementing the diet with vitamins and/or an internal skin and coat food supplement, and regular brushing are the basis for a healthy, shining coat. A bristle brush is the best choice for short-haired breeds. Always use a brush with medium/soft bristles which will not scratch the dog's skin but will remove the dead hair and scurf. Before brushing, spray the coat with an aerosol conditioner to prevent dryness and add sheen.

Use the brush first against the growth of the hair, from the tail to the head, as shown in Photograph 30, to remove as much dead hair as possible. Then brush in the opposite direction, from head to tail, and down the legs to smooth the coat. On short-haired breeds with large eyes, do not use a bristle brush on the head area. Instead, brush the head and ears with the soft rubber brush described in the Equipment Chapter, as shown in Photograph 31.

Brushing Toy Spaniels

Japanese Spaniel, Cavalier King Charles Spaniel, English Toy Spaniel

Place the dog on the grooming table. Spray the hair lightly with an aerosol conditioner or coat dressing. Use a small pin or natural bristle brush. Brush the body coat in layers with the growth of hair. Use a long, sweeping stroke that goes beyond the ends of the coat to avoid breaking off the hair tips. Brush the long feathering on the front of the chest in layers. Begin close to the front legs and work upward, letting your free hand separate the unbrushed hair from the section that is being brushed. Brush the long feathering on the tail, legs and ears downward.

The correct comb for Toy Spaniels is the half-fine, half-medium comb described in the Equipment Chapter. After the hair has been brushed, use the medium side of the comb through the coat to be sure all mats and tangles are removed.

Brushing the Pet Bichon Frise and Pet Toy Poodle

The correct brush for pet Bichons and Toy Poodles is the slicker brush described in the Equipment Chapter. Stand the dog on the grooming table. Start at the back of the dog and brush towards the front. Brush the back legs first, using a downward stroke, as shown in Photograph 32. Notice that the hair is parted to the skin and the free hand holds the unbrushed hair down, separating it from the portion being brushed. Holding the back leg in the position shown in Photograph 33, brush upward, using brisk strokes that lift the hair rather than flatten it. Continue working forward and brush the tail, hindquarters, back, ribs and chest, parting the hair and brushing to the skin, as shown in Photograph 34.

Turn the dog around to stand facing you to brush out the front of the chest. Gently pull each front leg forward and brush upward, as shown in Photograph 35. Place the dog in a sitting position, facing you and brush the topknot hair upward and backward. Brush the ear feathering downward (Photograph 36).

After the hair is completely brushed, comb through the coat to be sure all tangles are removed. Photograph 37 shows the Bichon Frise brushed and combed.

For the longer show coat, use a pin or natural bristle brush and brush the hair in layers, as described next.

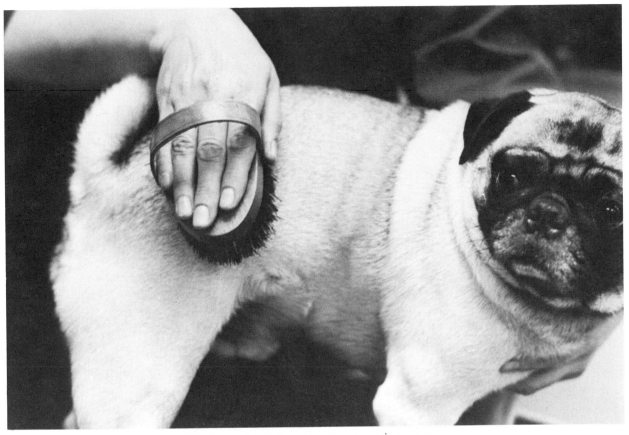

Photograph 30. Brushing the short-haired dog.

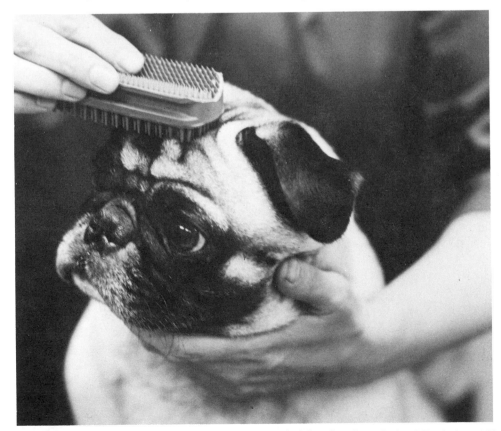

Photograph 31. The rubber brush is recommended for the short-haired Toy's head if he is of a breed with large, prominent eyes.

23

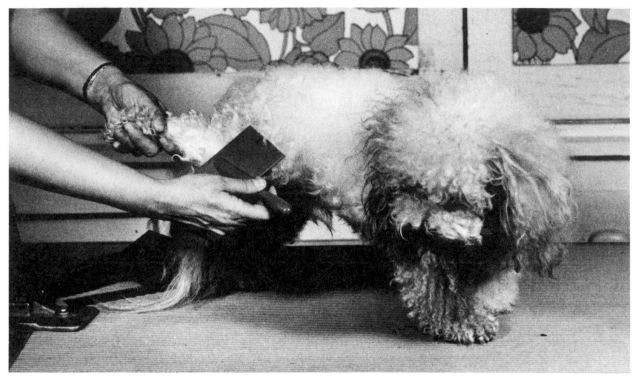

Photograph 32. The hindleg is held in this position during the brushing operation. Remember to lift the hair while you brush it.

Photograph 33. It is a good idea to hold the unbrushed hair with your free hand and brush in layers the hair you are working with.

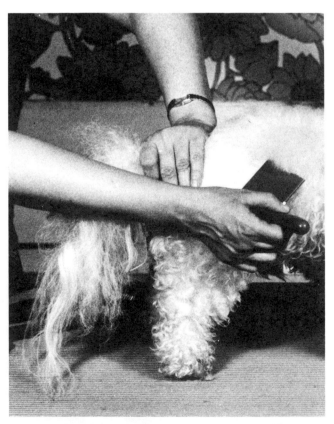

Photograph 34. Brush from back to front, making sure you get right down to the skin.

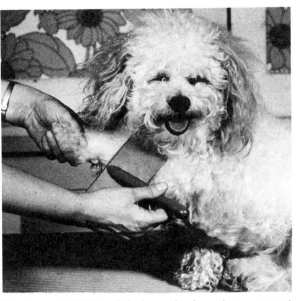

Photograph 35. Brush hair on the front legs upward. Bichons and Toy Poodles should have a full, fluffy look when groomed. So, work with this effect in mind.

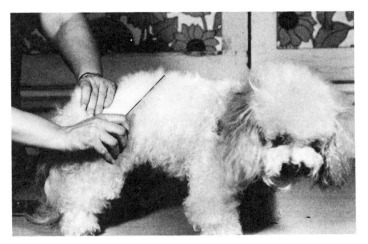

Photograph 36. After thorough brushing, comb through the coat to make sure all snarls have been removed.

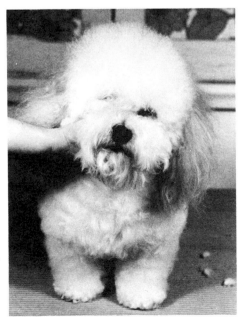

Photograph 37. A front view of the fully groomed Bichon Frise. The full, plushy coat is not difficult to maintain, but does require regular grooming to keep it right.

Brushing the Long, Flowing Coated Breeds

Maltese, Lhasa Apso, Shih Tzu, Silky Terrier, Yorkshire Terrier, Tibetan Terrier.

The above mentioned breeds all have long coats of various textures which hang flat over the sides of the body, falling straight down to the ground in most instances. This type of long coat must be brushed at least three times per week to keep the hair free of tangles. To thoroughly brush a long, flowing coated dog, the hair must be brushed in layers from the skin out. Each layer is moistened with a coat dressing or aerosol coat conditioner before it is brushed. Never brush a dry coat. This causes static electricity which will damage and break off the ends of the hair.

All of the above mentioned breeds have an abundance of hair around the mouth. If there is an accumulation of food or dirt caked in the beard, before you begin brushing, put some liquid tangle remover on the beard and work it into the hair with your fingers. While you brush the long body coat, the tangle remover will loosen any mats or food that have caked in the hair.

The correct brush for the long, flowing coated breeds is a pin brush, a natural bristle brush or a very fine quality nylon bristle brush. All three types of brushes are described in the Equipment Chapter. A slicker brush may be used on the feet, if necessary.

Begin by brushing the hair under the chest. On a toy dog, the easiest way to do this is to sit in a chair, spreading a towel over your legs. Place the dog on its back on your lap, as shown in Photograph 38. Many pets are not accustomed to this brushing method and may struggle when you first turn them over but, by holding the dog gently and speaking quietly and reassuringly, the dog will learn to relax. To brush the hair under the chest on the Lhasa Apso and Tibetan Terrier, have the dog lie on the grooming table and lift the front leg.

Spread the long body coat out to the sides (this will be brushed later when the dog is in another position) and spray the hair with a light oil or coat dressing. Using the pin or bristle brush, begin at the stomach and work up to the front legs, brushing the hair in layers from the skin out, as shown in Photograph 39. This area is often the most tangled and you may need to respray each layer of hair with conditioner as you brush. While the dog is in this position, be sure to brush any hard-to-get areas under the front legs. After the chest hair is brushed, comb through the coat, as shown in Photograph 40, to be sure all tangles are removed.

Now brush the body coat. Place the dog on its side with feet facing you on the grooming table. If your pet dog refuses to lie still on the table, allow him to stand for layer brushing, although it is a bit more difficult to accomplish in the standing position. Begin near the chest and make a part in the coat the entire length of the body parallel with the backbone, down to the skin, as shown in Photograph 41. The hair can be parted lengthwise with the edge of a comb or a knitting needle. Spray the hair above and below the part line with a coat conditioner or coat dressing and brush downward from the part line. The correct brush stroke is long and sweeping, going beyond the ends of the hair to prevent damage or breakage of the hair ends. Hold the brush loosely in your hand, allowing the handle to swing like a metronome. Eventually, with a little practice, you will develop a light, rotary wrist action that allows you to brush long, flowing coats without tiring and with very little hair loss.

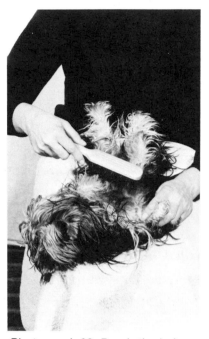

Photograph 38. It is often advisable to have the dog in your lap to brush undersides, legs and armpits of Toy dogs with long, flowing coats.

Photograph 39. Brush the hair on the underside in layers, making sure all tangles are removed. Use of a conditioner is very desirable for this work.

Photograph 40. Comb through the coat on the underside. Any tangles which withstood the brush should now be dealt with.

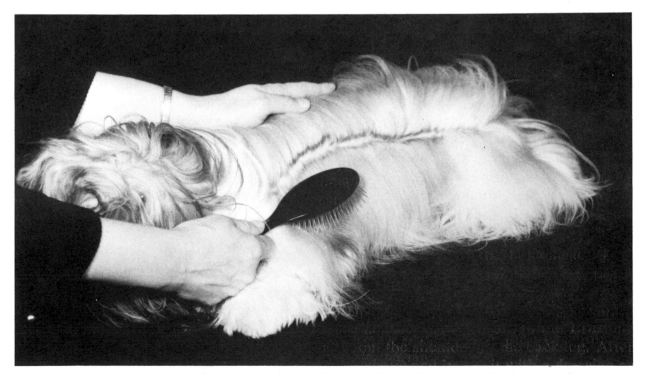

Photograph 41. The first step in brushing the body of a flowing-coated dog is to part the coat as shown above. Use a pin brush for this.

Next, make another part lengthwise about one inch above the hair you have just brushed and, once again, spray and brush this hair section straight down, as shown in Photograph 42. Work upward in layers, spraying and brushing until you reach the center of the back, then turn the dog over and brush the other side the same way.

Brush the leg hairs in layers (Photograph 43). If the feet are matted or dirty, brush lightly with a slicker brush.

Sit the dog on the table facing you. The hair on the front of the chest is brushed in layers. Begin close to the front legs and work upward, as shown in Photograph 44. Brush the tail against the growth (Photograph 45).

Brushing the Head

Brush the hair on the top of the head away from the eyes, as shown in Photograph 46. Brush the hair on the sides of the head and around the mouth, taking care not to injure the eyes with the bristles or pins on the brush. Brush the ear feathering downward.

Combing the Long, Flowing Coated Breeds

The correct comb for the long, flowing coated breeds is the half-fine, half-medium tooth comb described in the Equipment Chapter. After the hair has been brushed thoroughly, comb through the coat with the medium side of the comb to be sure all mats have been removed. Always use the comb in a gentle manner to avoid pulling out the undercoat. Photograph 47 shows the use of the extra-fine tooth comb removing matter near the corners of the eyes. Photograph 48 shows the use of the same comb removing food particles from the beard. If you have soaked the beard hair before starting to brush, this hair should comb out easily. Do not tug through the coat with the fine-tooth comb or you may pull out more hair than necessary.

Matting in Long, Flowing Coated Breeds

If a long, flowing coat is badly matted, the groomer may need to use a slicker brush to remove the tangles. Photograph 49 shows a side view and Photograph 50 shows a front view of a matted Lhasa Apso pet which could never be brushed out with the pin brush because the tangles are so heavy. On this type of coat, a slicker is necessary to remove mats. Brush with light strokes, taking care not to use too much pressure with the slicker. Using a heavy stroke can scratch the dog's delicate skin. Soak the hair thoroughly with a liquid tangle remover before brushing and follow instructions for brushing found in the "Coat Problems" Chapter.

Brushing Other Toy Breeds

Directions for brushing all other toy breeds will be found in the grooming chapter for each breed.

Note: Every dog should have its own brush. However, if you have a grooming shop, kennel or own many dogs and, for economy's sake, must use the same brush on more than one dog, it should be cleaned thoroughly before each use on a different dog. Skin disease and parasites can be spread rapidly by using the same brush on several dogs

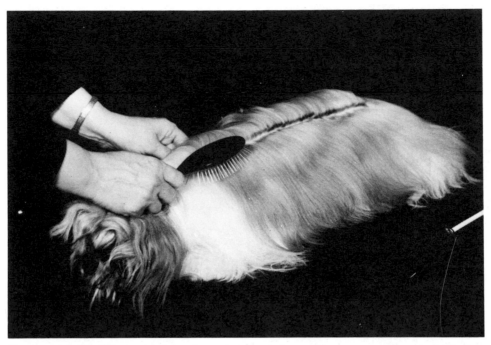

Photograph 42. When you have layer brushed the entire coat, make a straight part down the length of the back. Spray the part with a conditioner to keep it in place.

Photograph 43. Brush leg furnishings in layers similar to the way the body coat is handled.

Photograph 44. Start brushing the chest just above the front legs and work upward in layers.

Photograph 45. The tail, like the rest of the body, must be free of all snarls. It is finished in breeds like Shih Tzu by being brushed toward the head.

Photograph 46. When brushing the long furnishings of the head in the flowing-coated breeds take care not to damage the often-prominent eyes.

without cleaning it. When a dirty coat is pre-brushed before bathing, remember to wash the brush before using it again on the clean dog.

Slicker and pin brushes are easy to clean. Fill a little plastic pan with liquid detergent and warm water. Plunge the brush into the water and swish it around. Then hold the brush under the faucet and rinse. Dry thoroughly. Bristle brushes should be soaked in warm, soapy water for a few minutes, swished around, rinsed well and dried.

In a grooming shop, brushes, combs and clipper blades which have been used on dogs with skin disease or parasites must be cleaned in a germicide/sterilizer solution. Most of these solutions contain an anti-rust agent, allowing you to sterilize equipment as often as you wish.

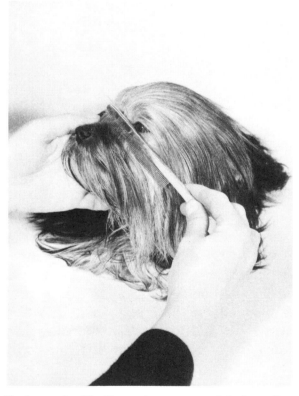

Photograph 47. Removing accumulated matter from eye corners is best accomplished with a flea comb.

Photograph 48. The flea comb is also used to remove dried food particles that have adhered to the beard. You may have to soak this furnishing in a tangle remover before combing.

Coat Problems

Facts About Matted Hair

All long-haired dogs get mats if they are incorrectly brushed. A common error is to select the right brush for your dog, then use it to brush the top coat only and assume that the job is thorough. This usually results in the dog becoming one solid block of matting next to the skin. Large mats can be difficult to remove, for no dog can be expected to sit quietly while you pull through the coat trying to remove tangles.

There are critical "coat matting" periods for long-haired dogs. The most difficult period is when the dog is about one year old and the puppy coat is changing to adult texture. At this time, the top coat is rather sparse and the hair near the skin much thicker. If the dog is not brushed every day or every other day, the hair mats together and forms large clumps near the skin which are impossible to get out. If the coat is neglected during this critical period, the dog may have to be cut down.

Long periods of damp weather and humidity make the hair mat easily. Winter weather is harsh on long-coated dogs. Pets that are allowed to romp in the snow and become soaking wet tend to mat easily if the coat is not brushed and dried properly afterward.

Brushing Matted Hair

Using a liquid tangle remover, saturate all matted areas and allow the product to remain on the hair until almost dry. Begin mat removal by breaking apart large mats and separating them into smaller sections. This can be done with the Oliver Mat Splitter or a rake, a special grooming tool with two rows of diagonally set teeth with rounded ends which will not scratch the dog's skin. After each section is separated, use the brush through the hair. When working on damaged or matted hair, always use a protein conditioner between groomings. Rather than just coating the hair with an attractive sheen for a few days, the protein is absorbed into the hair and repairs the damaged hair shaft. The long-term benefits show up after weeks of regular use—the coat builds up strength and is thicker in texture.

Removing Mats from the Show Coat

With a little patience, even the largest mat can be removed from a show coat with little hair loss. The first step is to spray the dog with a protein aerosol conditioner as

Photograph 49. This extremely matted Lhasa Apso will have to undergo many arduous hours of grooming to relieve his pitiful condition. Regular grooming and coat care could have easily avoided this dog's present condition.

suggested above, or a liquid tangle removing preparation. After spraying, work the product into the matted areas with your fingers and allow it to remain on the hair for at least 1/2 hour.

Large mats in a show coat should be gently untangled, rather than pulled or cut out. Begin by separating and isolating the mat from the rest of the long coat. Use your fingers to gently work the mat apart and separate it into two smaller sections.

Next, use the rake or mat splitter to break up the two matted sections into four smaller sections. At this point, the hair may need to be dampened again with the tangle remover. Keep separating each section into smaller sections, then use a pin or bristle brush to brush out each tiny mat.

Emergency Coat Saving Hints:

TO REMOVE BEARD AND MOUSTACHE STAINS, TO DRYCLEAN COAT: Use Ring 5 Whitener-Cleaner. Spray on hair, wait a few minutes, then brush out.

TO REMOVE GRASS AND UNDERBODY STAINS: Use Ring 5 Whitener-Cleaner. Spray on hair, wait about 5 minutes, then brush out.

TO REMOVE EXCESSIVE STAINS FROM BEARD HAIR: Saturate stained hair with ginger ale. Let dry, then wash out of hair.

ITCHING, SCRATCHING, MINOR SKIN IRRITATIONS, INSECT BITES, SUNBURN, SUPERFICIAL CUTS AND SCRATCHES: Use Cortisynth Cream or spray affected area with Ring 5 Medicated Spray. If irritation is severe or problems persist, consult veterinarian.

33

Photograph 50. When faced with a seriously matted dog, the groomer and the dog may be better off with using a slicker brush to help untangle the coat. Some dogs are so badly matted they must be clipped down to skin and grow an all-new coat.

Photograph 51. A liquid detangler is often helpful in undoing matted coats. For best results always follow manufacturer's directions.

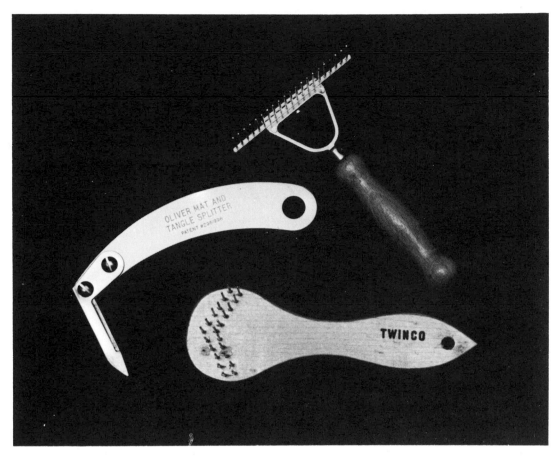

Photograph 52. The grooming tools above are especially designed to break apart mats. Used correctly they can make the unpleasant task of removing mats faster and easier for all concerned.

BURRS: Saturate burrs with mineral or baby oil. The coat will become slippery and burrs will brush out easily.

CHEWING GUM: Rub peanut butter into the gum, let stand a few minutes, then comb out of coat. Another way to remove chewing gum is to rub an ice cube over the gum. It will become brittle and easy to pull out of the hair.

GREASE SPOTS: Use Ring 5 Whitener-Cleaner or Fuller's Earth. Dust into coat. Leave on for about one hour, brush out, shampoo and rinse thoroughly. Repeat if necessary.

SKUNK OR FERTILIZER ODOR: Rub tomato juice (or vanilla extract) into coat. Leave on for about one hour, then shampoo and rinse thoroughly. Repeat if necessary.

TAR IN FEET OR COAT: Soak tarred area in warm water. Then soak the same area in mineral oil. Repeat above until the tar loosens and works out of the coat. Or, rub Crisco into the tarred areas and let it remain in the hair until the tar softens. Shampoo twice and rinse well. Both methods may have to be repeated for stubborn cases.

DOG CHEWING COAT: Assuming there is nothing physically wrong with the dog and that he may be chewing out of boredom, spray the hair with "Bitter Apple" or Capsicum.

How to Treat Stained Hair

Eye Stain

White and light-colored long-haired dogs, particularly Toy Poodles, Maltese, Shih Tzu, Lhasa Apsos and Bichon Frises, often have dark stains under the eyes caused by a discharge from the tear ducts. These tear stains discolor the hair and leave unsightly reddish-brown stains, often creating the effect of dark circles under the eyes. Eyestain is caused by many different reasons—heredity, teething, improper diet, neglect in grooming or infection of the tear ducts.

Whatever the cause, if your dog has noticeable eye stain, it becomes a problem to keep the face clean. Nothing looks worse than a beautiful long-coated dog with a neglected, stained face. Many pet owners are unaware of how to cope with eye stain, consequently their dogs are often neglected between groomings.

Daily attention to the eye area is the best way to control eyestain. First, comb the hair under the eyes with a fine-tooth comb to clean away any accumulated matter. Next, a soothing eye lotion, such as Eye Brite, should be dropped into each eye. When doing this, also apply a few drops of Eye-Brite to the stained areas below the eyes to help neutralize and remove the discoloration.

For extreme cases of eye stain, the following additional steps will help camouflage the discolorations:

Photograph 53. An unclipped white Toy Poodle. Notice the excessive stains on the long hairs under the eyes.

Photograph 54. Before camouflaging. The hair under the eyes has been clipped, washed with a tearless shampoo, rinsed and dried.

Photograph 55. To camouflage the stain, use Lambert-Kay's Eyetek, a siliconized chalk available in white, blond or silver stick form. Pencil the Eyetek onto the stained hair under each eye, then blend with your fingers until the stain disappears. This product blushes easily to match the dog's natural coat color and you can use two colors together to achieve maximum results, i.e., white first, then blond overtop, or white with silver on top.

Photograph 56. The finished results. Once applied, Eyetek leaves a silicone coating to retard further staining, allowing the hair to return to normal color.

Photograph 53. This white Toy Poodle displays very badly neglected eye stains. Eye stain can be a problem with white or light-colored, long-haired dogs. It is usually a result of individual hairs coming to rest on the cornea. The resultant irritation triggers a tearing reflex and the tears, left unchecked, cause the unsightly staining.

Photograph 54. This is the same dog as in photo 53. The face has been clipped, but the deep stains are as obvious and as ugly as before.

37

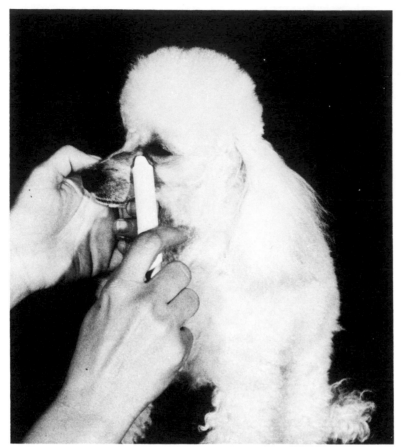

Photograph 55. After clipping, siliconized chalk is applied to the stained areas of the face. This specially formulated chalk is available in several colors and has a blusher to help blend into the natural coat color. The silicones also help to retard further staining.

Caution: On the above mentioned breeds, never cut out large clumps of stained hair around the eyes to improve the dog's appearance. When the hair grows back, the ends will curl into the eyes and further aggravate the tearing condition. Also, on breeds with tied-up forelocks (Maltese, Shih Tzu, Lhasa Apso, etc.) be sure that the wisps of forelocks do not fall into the eyes to cause additional tearing. If the forelocks do not hold in place with a rubber band, cut a two inch square of white nylon tulle. Part the forelocks as usual, wrap the tulle around the hair, gathering all wispy ends under the tulle, then fasten back as usual with the rubber band.

Beard Stains

The light-colored dogs mentioned above, plus the Yorkshire Terrier, Silky Terrier, Tibetan Terrier and Brussels Griffon, have an abundance of facial furnishings. The long hair around the mouth often becomes discolored, usually from food or foreign matter caking in the hair. In some cases of extreme neglect, the hair becomes so badly discolored that the stain cannot be removed completely.

Daily care will help control the stain and keep it from reaching the "impossible to remove" stage. The hair around the mouth should be combed to remove all traces of food or dirt caked in the coat. Afterwards, use one of the following methods to remove beard stains:

Method 1. Spot clean the beard hair with a whitener shampoo. Rinse well and dry. If you are careful, you can wash the head area without wetting the body hair.

Method 2. Spray beard stains with Ring 5 Whitener-Cleaner. Allow the powder to

Photograph 56. The eye stains have been completely covered and the dog's appearance much improved. Eye stain is a recurring problem, however and the dog who has it once will have it again unless constant eye care is used.

remain in the hair for a few minutes, then brush out. When spraying beard hair, be sure to cover the eyes with your free hand.

Method 3. Severe stains can be toned down by using one of the following mixtures:

(a) 1/2 cup Fuller's Earth
    1/2 cup Cornstarch

(b) 1/3 cup Cornstarch
    1/3 cup Silicone Grooming Powder For Dogs
    1/3 cup French White Chalk Powder

Mix either formulation in a plastic container with a lid. Mix more than you need for one application and keep the lid on the container. The powder will not get dirty and is always ready for future use. Apply by wetting the stained area around the beard with warm water. Then use fingers, a dog chalk brush or small human complexion brush, and put the mixture on the wet area until a thick "paste" forms. Allow the paste and hair to dry, then brush out with a soft brush. If you are a professional groomer, apply the paste immediately after the shampoo and final rinse. Just dry the legs, body and tail first while the paste hardens, then dry the head area last. On show dogs, many exhibitors leave the paste in the hair overnight, then brush it out the next morning. This method can be used two to three times per week, if necessary.

Underbody Stains and Grass Stains on Dogs

On many white and light-colored long-haired toy dogs, the underbody and leg feathering becomes stained when a male lifts his leg to urinate. In addition to causing unattractive yellow stains, the dried urine damages the hair shaft, making it dry, brittle and easily susceptible to breakage. A long, light-colored coat can also be stained or damaged by prolonged contact to grass and weeds. These can be serious problems for the owner of a show dog, where long feathering is necessary for competition.

Before treating the stain, you must condition the brittle ends of the coat to prevent breakage. This can be done by using an aerosol coat conditioner with protein. Protein products help to rebuild and strengthen the structure of the hair. From a grooming standpoint, most dog coat conditioners or coat dressings function only on the outer layer of the hair without penetrating the shaft. Protein, on the other hand, is readily absorbed into the hair shaft to help rebuild and gradually thicken the hair. Since a dog's hair is mostly protein in content, when the coat is damaged, you want to fortify it with some of the essential elements you have lost, i.e., more protein. For fast action in extreme cases of damage, it may be necessary to use a human hair conditioner formulated specifically to treat damaged hair. Always apply the product by following package directions carefully.

Once the brittle ends have been conditioned to retard breakage, bathe the hair with a whitener shampoo, rinse well and dry as usual. To prevent stained underbody hair in between shampoos, several times a week, spray all areas susceptible to stain with Ring 5 Whitener/Cleaner. Allow the powder to remain in the coat for about ten minutes, then brush out with a soft brush.

Care of the Nails

A dog's nails should be cut each time he is groomed. If you intend to show your dog in the breed ring, the nails must be kept short at all times (with the exception of the Chihuahua) to keep the feet tight. On pet or show dog, nails that are neglected and allowed to grow long will make the feet spread, causing poor posture and eventually lameness. Most dogs detest having their nails clipped, but if you start trimming the nails when your dog is young, he will learn to accept this part of grooming. Never be angry or impatient with a frightened dog. Treat him gently and you will win his confidence. Use either of the following two methods to shorten the nails:

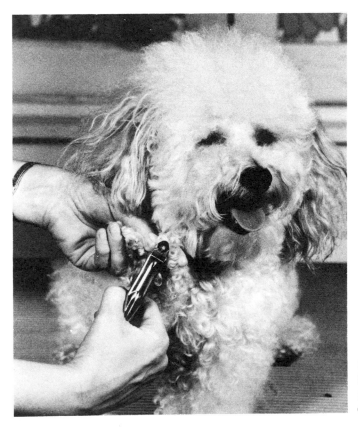

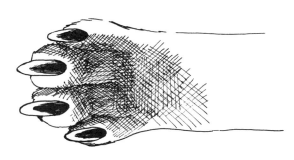

Diagram 1. There is a vein present in each nail on the dog's foot. Great care should be taken in cutting and filing operations, not to sever this. Profuse bleeding and considerable pain to the dog will result if this vein or quick is cut.

Photograph 57. With the exception of the Chihuahua all dogs require to have well-trimmed nails. Short nails not only look better, but are essential to strong feet and good posture.

Method A: Nail Clippers and File

Place the dog in a sitting position, facing you. It is important that you have proper control over the dog. Hold the foot in your free hand, gently pulling it forward. Place the nail trimmer in the palm of your hand and insert the nail into the opening above the cutting blade, as shown in Photograph 57. Press the trimmer together and cut each nail back a little at a time, stopping when you reach the "quick," a tender fleshy area inside the nail shown in Diagram 1. Cutting into the quick will make the nail bleed. If this happens, moisten a cotton ball with Clip Stop or Monsel's Powder and press it firmly against the nail for a minute to stop the bleeding. The quick is easily seen on white and light-colored dogs, but on dark dogs you must try to locate it from the underside of each nail before you begin cutting.

After the nails have been cut back, use a nail file to smooth any rough edges. File in one direction only, from the top of the nail downward.

Method B: Electric Nail Sander

Place the dog in a sitting position, facing you. Hold the foot in your free hand, gently pulling it forward. Place the side of the sanding disc on the side of the nail and roll it back and forth across the nail to shorten it. A word of caution: electric nail sanders operate at a high speed and shorten the nails quickly. Always use the sander in short rolling strokes. Never press for a long time in one spot on the nail because the high speed sander gets very hot. If you are working on a long-haired dog with an abundance of hair around the foot or on the leg, hold the sander close to the nails and not near the long hair while the motor is running. The sander could get tangled in the coat and pull out hair. Also, be careful that the dog does not put his head down to see what you are doing while the sander is running. The long ear fringes could get tangled in the sander, causing the dog great pain. If you are working on a fidgety dog, it would help to have an assistant hold the dog firmly so he cannot put his head down or move his legs around.

Care of the Eyes

Many long-haired breeds need regular eye care, particularly those having an abundance of facial hair, such as the Maltese, Yorkshire Terrier, Shih Tzu, Bichon Frise, Lhasa Apso, etc. In addition, many toy breeds such as the Pekingese, Brussels Griffon, Chihuahua, Pug, Shih Tzu and the Toy Spaniels have large, round eyes which are set in shallow sockets. Because these eyes are not as protected as the smaller type, they are extremely sensitive and need constant care. They should be washed daily and kept free of mucous matter. Any accumulation of mucous or dirt makes the dog rub its eyes; the cornea may be injured and ulceration may result. On these breeds, the eyes can be scratched and ulcerated easily from a number of causes: playing, ingrown eye lashes which irritate the eyeball, or by hair in the eyes during the shedding period. If neglected, the eye may be permanently scarred or, worse yet, the dog may lose its sight.

Every day, the dog's eyes should be washed out with a soothing solution, such as Eye-Brite, designed to clean the eyes of dirt and other foreign particles. Eye-Brite is easy to use. With one hand, gently lift the dog's head upward and place a few drops of Eye-Brite into each eye. Place the drops in the eye to allow the Eye-Brite to flow across the eyeball into the corner of each eye. This will float any foreign matter to the corner of the eyes where it can be removed carefully with a Q-tip. Do not rub over the eyeball with cotton for you can scratch it and cause irritation! Wipe away any excess solution under the eyes with cotton or a tissue.

Air pollution is a serious problem today and, like humans, pets too are affected by foreign matter in the air. Eye-Brite can be used on all breeds to prevent minor irritations.

Never ignore eye problems. On all long-haired dogs, problems can be caused by shedding hair getting into the eyes or eyelashes which irritate the eyeball. The first signs of trouble are redness, blinking of the eyelids and persistent scratching by the dog. When this happens, consult your veterinarian and he will prescribe the proper ophthalmic ointment.

Caution: You can irritate a dog's eyes by improper grooming. Never use a stiff bristle, wire or pin brush in a careless manner on the head area of a toy dog with large, protruding eyes. Never spray aerosol products directly towards the face. If necessary, cover the eyes with your hand or, better yet, spray the contents onto your fingers, then rub the product into the facial hair.

Care of the Ears

Cleaning the ears is an important part of a dog's grooming routine. Short-haired small breeds rarely experience ear problems. All that is necessary to keep their ears in good condition is a swabbing at regular intervals to remove accumulations of dirt and prevent infection.

Many of the long-haired breeds have hair growing inside their ears which needs to be removed periodically. If the ears are attended to every month, they should remain in good condition and the cleaning will take only a short time. But if the hair is neglected and allowed to grow long, especially on the heavy-coated breeds with hanging ears, wax will accumulate in the hair, cut off air circulation and eventually cause infection and canker. The most common reason for neglecting to clean a dog's ears seems to be a lack of understanding of the ear canal and the proper way to remove the hair by the novice groomer.

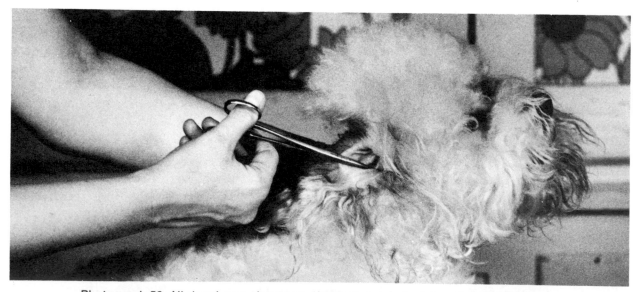

Photograph 58. All dogs' ears should be checked at regular intervals and cleaned as needed. In long-haired breeds, hair grows inside the ear canal and should be regularly plucked out.

How to Clean the Ears

The first step in cleaning the ears is to remove any long hair leading into the ear canal. Always do this job on a sturdy grooming table in a room with adequate light. Sit the dog on the table. Shake a small amount of ear powder into each ear. Ear powders formulated especially for dogs are available at your local pet shop. Powdering the ears makes plucking easier and faster by giving you a better grip on the hair. Using your thumb and index finger or a Kelly Fine Point Forceps, as shown in Photograph 58, pull out the excess hair leading into the ear canal. Gently pull out a few hairs at a time, otherwise it will be painful to your dog.

When the excess hair has been removed, insert a few drops of a canine ear solution into the ear. Use a Q-tip to carefully clean the area that you can see. Do not probe into the ear canal!

If there is an excessive wax accumulation deep inside the ear canal, insert a few drops of the ear lotion into the canal. Drop the medication into the ear by pulling the ear out, away from the head, to make the opening into the canal as large as possible. Then massage the base of the ear to loosen the wax and make it float to the surface. Use dry cotton to absorb the accumulation until the canal is clean and dry. There are many excellent ear lotions for dogs, formulated to clean the ear and soften wax. Most of these products are insecticidal to help destroy ear mites and bactericidal to help prevent infection.

Dogs that are prone to severe and chronic ear infections and accumulate excessive amounts of wax deep inside the ear should be attended to by a veterinarian. If you notice your dog shaking its head and scratching the ears, or if the ears have a foul odor and reddish-brown discharge, seek professional attention immediately.

Care of the Teeth

All dogs have two sets of teeth, the baby or "milk" teeth and the permanent teeth. A few days after birth, the puppy teeth start to appear. By one month, the puppy should have all of its baby teeth, 28 in all. There are 14 teeth in the lower and upper jaws—6 incisors, 2 canines and 6 premolars.

Between 10 weeks and 4 months, the baby teeth begin falling out and are replaced by permanent teeth. The upper incisors usually come in first, the molars last. An adult dog should have 42 teeth. There are 20 in the upper jaw (6 incisors, 2 canines, 4 premolars and 4 molars) and 22 in the lower jaw (6 incisors, 2 canines, 4 premolars and 6 molars).

A close check must be kept on teething puppies. Occasionally, permanent teeth appear before the baby teeth fall out and the dog may have two teeth in the same spot. Puppy teeth that do not fall out should be removed, as they may cause misplacement of the permanent teeth. If you want to show your puppy, regularly check the mouth for "double teeth" (i.e., baby tooth and adult tooth in the same spot). Double teeth can cause serious problems in teeth alignment and ruin the adult bite. If double teeth occur, ask your veterinarian to remove the baby tooth so the permanent bite will not be spoiled. If you are a novice, do not attempt to pull a baby tooth yourself. The jaws of a toy dog are delicate and may be dislocated or broken by exerting pressure.

Periodically, the teeth should be cleaned by rubbing them with a moist cloth that has been dipped into a mixture of equal parts baking soda and salt.

Just like a human being, softness or brittleness in a dog's teeth is hereditary. Toy dogs seem to suffer with soft and defective teeth far more than the larger breeds, even though they have been fed a well-balanced diet. Soft teeth tend to quickly accumulate tartar around the gum line. If the tartar is neglected, a brown crust-like substance grows on the tooth near the gums. Eventually, bacteria lodge under the gums and they thicken and recede from around the tooth. To keep the teeth and gums healthy and free from infection, tartar must be scraped off. This is not a pleasant job to do, since no dog enjoys having his teeth scraped. Many people prefer to let their veterinarian remove the tartar.

Removing Tartar from the Teeth

If you do wish to scrape the tartar from your dog's teeth, you will need a dental scaler with right and left angles. If a dental scaler is not available at your local pet shop, ask your dentist to order one for you.

Place your dog on a sturdy grooming table. Begin by scraping the tartar from the top teeth. Place the sharp part of your scaler up under the gum line, then scrape downward, using your free thumb to shield the gums and lips below. Tartar does not seem to accumulate as heavily on the bottom teeth, but if it is necessary to scrape these teeth, place the edge of the scaler slightly under the gum line and scrape upward, using your thumb to shield the upper teeth. Pushing the scaler under the gum line and scraping the teeth usually makes the gums bleed. After the tartar is removed, moisten a cotton swab with merthiolate and paint the gums to prevent infection. Disinfect your scaler before and after you use it.

Once the tartar is scraped off and the teeth clean, a product called "Happy Breath" will prevent tartar from forming again, if used daily according to package directions. "Happy Breath" is a special dog dentifrice that comes in an easy-to-use plastic squeeze bottle. In addition to softening tartar, it destroys mouth bacteria and keeps the dog's breath pleasant smelling.

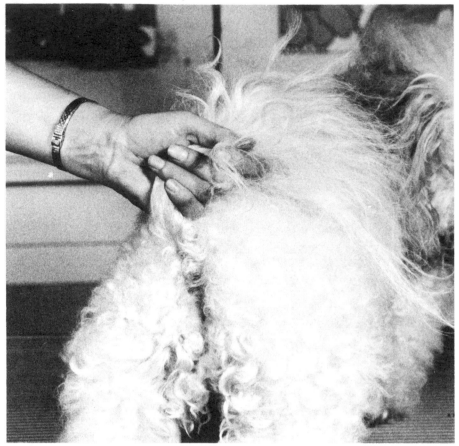

Photograph 59. Have the dog on a raised surface and in the position shown when preparing to express anal glands. The secretion is extremely malodorous, and lack of control can make for a messy situation. Many people prefer to take care of glands as part of the dog's bath.

Photograph 60. Have a large wad of cotton, tissue or paper towel against the anal opening and squeeze the glands together gently. With most dogs the accumulated material should come out easily.

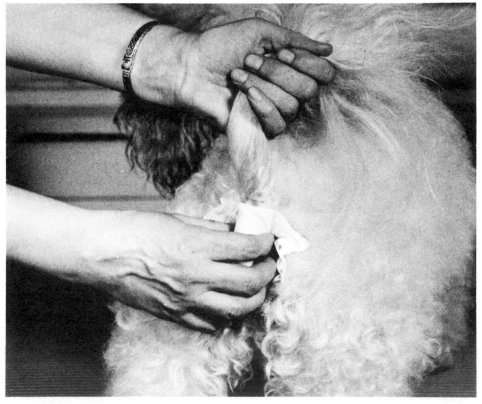

The Anal Glands

Every dog has a pair of anal glands, located on the sides of and just below the opening to the anus. These glands secrete a brownish-yellow fluid which empties into the anus. The exact function of the anal glands is often disputed. Some experts say that they secrete a lubricant to help the dog move its bowels easily. Others believe that the anal glands are vestigal musk glands left over from the dog's primitive state, which once functioned like those of a skunk to frighten away possible attackers. To be sure, the skunk's musk glands are located in the same spot as the dog's anal glands and the secretion from the skunk's glands is similar to that of the dog except for the intensity of odor.

Sometimes the anal glands become clogged and accumulate a foul-smelling mass inside. This leads to an irritation which the dog tries to relieve by pulling himself across the floor on his hindquarters or by licking and biting at the base of the tail. Eventually, an abscess which is quite painful to the dog may develop. When this happens, the dog becomes listless, his eyes appear dull and he often refuses to eat and becomes constipated. On examination, the anus appears inflamed and you may even notice the skin bulging over the glands. Anal gland impaction is common in toy dogs, probably because they are fed softer food than the larger breeds. Larger dogs eat bulkier foods which produce stiffer fecal matter to aid in preventing clogged anal glands.

Veterinarians state that a large number of dogs that are brought in for treatment have impacted anal glands and the owners are completely unaware of what the problem is. Usually, when the dog starts scooting across the floor on his haunches, the owner consults a veterinarian, thinking his dog has worms.

Periodically, the anal glands should be checked for impaction. How often you need to do this depends on the frequency of accumulation in each dog, and the anal glands seem to be different in all dogs. Some dogs need monthly attention, others may go from two to three months without any accumulation and many dogs never need to have the anal glands emptied.

When clogged glands are suspected, they must be squeezed to discharge the accumulation inside. Expressing the anal glands is not a pleasant job, but it has to be done to prevent further infection.

If you are going to bathe the dog, check the glands immediately before putting the dog in the tub, or do it just after you stand him in the water, since the accumulation is so foul-smelling.

To properly empty the anal glands, stand the dog on the grooming table (or in the tub). Hold the tail up with your hand, as shown in Photograph 59. Cover the anus with a piece of cotton, as the accumulation will spurt out when the glands are squeezed. Place the thumb and index finger of your other hand in the position shown in Photograph 60, gently squeeze the fingers together and the contents of the glands will squirt out onto the cotton. If the glands have been clogged for some time, the secretion may come out like toothpaste from a tube instead of spurting. Do remember to be gentle and not squeeze with a heavy hand. Usually, when the glands are clogged, just the slightest pressure will release the fluid. However, some dogs have glands which can be difficult to express. Pressure has to be exerted in the right way to release the fluid. If this is the case, try getting your thumb and first finger under and firmly in back of the glands, then gently squeeze in an upward and outward motion.

If the dog is not to be bathed and there is an odor about the anus after the glands have been squeezed, moisten some fresh cotton with alcohol or warm, soapy water and clean the skin and hair.

As mentioned before, the color of the normal secretion is brownish-yellow. If pus or blood is noticed on the cotton, the dog should be taken to a veterinarian where, in cases of serious infection, antibiotics will be injected into the glands.

It should be pointed out that long-haired breeds such as the Maltese, Yorkshire Terrier, Shih Tzu, Pekingese, Pomeranian, Bichon Frise, Lhasa Apso and others with an abundance of hair around the anus, sometimes suffer from outside impaction. If the dog has a soft bowel movement, some of it might cling to the hair around the anus and form a mass. This mass will harden and seal the anal opening so securely making another bowel movement impossible. If not attended to immediately, the dog will bite this area and cause it to bleed. To remedy this situation, soak the tangled hair in warm water until the mass softens and can be removed. Shampoo and dry the stained hair. When the hair and skin are dry, apply an antibiotic ointment, such as Lambert Kay's Cortisynth, to the area.

Bathing and Drying the Dog

Preparing for the Bath

Preparing the dog for a bath is as important as the bath itself. There are several time-consuming steps to be taken before the bath and these are most important to the health of the skin and coat.

First, the dog should be brushed thoroughly to the skin. Short-haired dogs should be brushed with a bristle brush to remove all scurf and dead hair. If the dog has long hair, it's best to remove tangles and mats before bathing. If you don't brush properly before shampooing, tangles and mats tend to clump together when the hair is wet. When shampoo is put on the hair, it is often difficult to rinse out. For badly matted dogs, refer to the section "Bathing Tangled Dogs" included in this chapter.

Equipment Needed

Next, you must gather together all the equipment and supplies you will need for the shampoo: a rubber mat for the bottom of the tub; spray hose; shampoo brush, sponge or washcloth; regular and/or tearless shampoo; creme rinse or tangle-free preparation; cotton; several clean bath towels and a hair dryer.

Selecting the Correct Shampoo

Always choose a mild shampoo which leaves the natural oils in the coat but removes the dirt. Today, because so many companies that manufacture dog shampoos have superior research facilities, there are a variety of top-quality products to choose from Ring 5, Dermocare, St. Aubrey, Oster and many other companies, some designed for all-purpose use and others for special situations or problems. The following suggestions will help you select the right shampoo for your breed:

PROTEIN AND/OR ALL-PURPOSE SHAMPOOS—These formulations are rich, all-purpose shampoos which clean beautifully and are safe for all types of coats. Those containing proteins help repair damaged hair and, with regular use, tend to thicken the texture of the coat.

TEARLESS SHAMPOOS—Formulated to be mild, tearless shampoos are safe for puppies and dogs with sensitive skins. These formulations are especially effective in preventing eye irritation on breeds with large eyes set in shallow sockets, such as the Pekingese, Pug, Shih Tzu, Toy Spaniels, Brussels Griffon, etc.

MEDICATED SHAMPOOS—These are formulated to help relieve itching, scaling, bacterial fungus and non-specific types of dermatitis.

FLEA & TICK SHAMPOOS—These are high quality, oil-based insecticidal shampoos formulated to rid the dog of external parasites. The effective killing ingredient in these shampoos is pyrethrins, a safe, highly effective, non-toxic pesticide. Flea and Tick Shampoos are effective against external parasites but, most important of all, they clean and beautify the coat. When used as directed, they are safe for puppies.

COLOR SHAMPOOS—Available for black, brown, silver or apricot dogs. These shampoos are not permanent dyes or color changers but effective formulations which enhance the natural coat color by removing the oxidation from the hair shaft, highlighting the natural coat colors, rather than altering them.

WHITENER SHAMPOOS—Formulated for use on white or silver colored dogs to brighten the coat color and help remove yellow discolorations. Excellent also for white parti-colored dogs.

TEXTURIZING SHAMPOOS—Formulated for coarse-haired breeds to build body and resiliency into the coat. Excellent for use on all soft-coated puppies when a firmer texture is desired.

CONDITIONER-RICH SHAMPOOS—These are rich shampoos containing special hair conditioning ingredients to add body, manageability and sheen. Especially recommended for the long, flowing coated breeds.

Beginning the Bath

After the dog has been brushed, take him out to relieve himself. Clean any dirty hairs off the grooming table and spread one large, thick bath towel on top. Place a clean brush and comb on the table, and have the hair dryer set up and ready to switch on as soon as the wet dog is placed on the table.

Where you bathe your dog depends on his size and your grooming area. Small and medium-sized dogs can be bathed easily in one side of a stationary tub. If you have a kennel, grooming shop or are a breeder/exhibitor with lots of dogs, it would be less tiring to have a junior-sized bath tub elevated waist high in your grooming room.

Professionals use different methods of bathing toy breeds. Some like to fill the tub with about 2 to 3 inches of warm water, add about 1/2 cup of shampoo, swirl it around to make the water sudsy and then stand the dog in the water. Others prefer putting the dog in the tub, wetting it down with the spray hose and let the water run free during the shampoo. Whichever method you choose is a matter of personal preference—either way will get the dog clean.

Before putting the dog into the water, be sure to plug the ears with cotton. If your dog has chronic ear trouble, make certain that no water gets into the ears to further irritate them by putting some vaseline on the end of the cotton that is inserted into the ear.

Attach the spray hose to the faucet and place the rubber mat in the bottom of the tub to keep the dog from slipping.

The Bath

Stand the dog in the tub. Wet the hair thoroughly except for the head and ears. If the dog has a thick coat, be sure to wet the hair to the skin. Many dogs get fidgety when they are put into water, so wear a large, plastic apron to keep yourself dry.

When the dog is wet all over, squeeze fresh shampoo on the hair and work from the back to the front of the dog, washing the tail, back, rear legs, stomach, shoulders, brisket, neck and front legs, as shown in Photograph 61. Don't be afraid to give a brisk shampoo by massaging the soap into the skin with your fingertips or the sponge. Don't forget to shampoo the area under the tail, using the sponge to clean any dirty spots, as shown in Photograph 62. Pay attention to the stubborn spots under the front and back legs and at the hock joints by using extra shampoo and the sponge. Many people like to check the anal glands at this point. Once any fluid has been squeezed with cotton, the unpleasant odor can be immediately washed away with soapy water.

By now, the only part that has not been shampooed is the head, which has purposely been left dry. Many dogs hate to have their heads washed, so if you save this part until last, the dog will be much less frightened. Wet the head and ears and wash these areas with the sponge or washcloth, taking care not to get soap into the eyes. To avoid eye irritation, always wash the head and face with a tearless dog shampoo. Do remember that many of the toy breeds (Brussels Griffon, Toy Spaniels, Pekingese, Pug, Shih Tzu) have large protruding eyes which are set in shallow sockets. These eyes can be irritated easily by getting soap into them. Wet the sponge and clean the muzzle. On toy breeds with abundant facial hair, scrub the areas around the mouth and under the eyes with a soft toothbrush, as shown in Photograph 63.

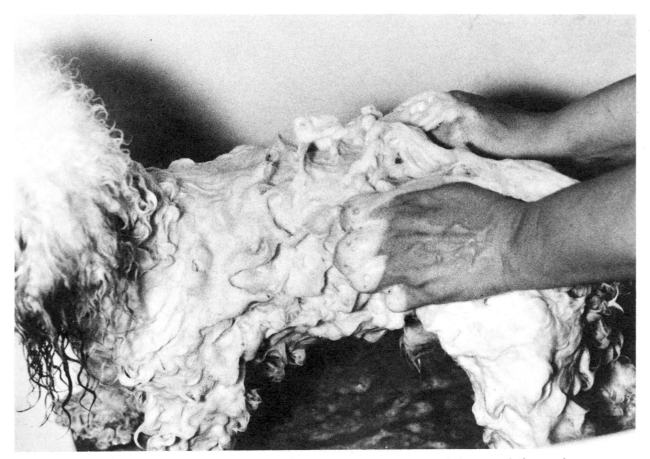

Photograph 61. After wetting the dog thoroughly, work up a good shampoo lather and soap the body thoroughly before going on to the head.

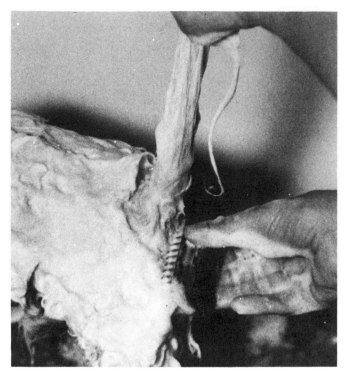

Photograph 62. If the dog's rear is stained, scrub the area carefully with the rubber brush or a sponge.

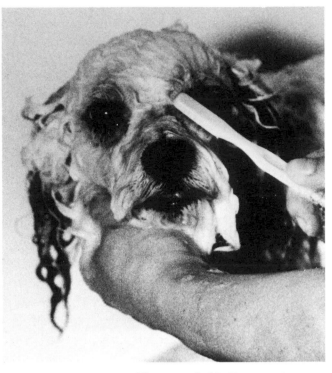

Photograph 63. Use a soft toothbrush around the eyes and the beards of long-haired Toys to remove as much stain as possible.

Photograph 64. In rinsing, deal with the head first and do not remove cotton plugs from the ears until the dog is out of the tub.

Photograph 65. Make certain every trace of shampoo is rinsed out of the coat before removing the dog from the tub. Any left-over shampoo residue will dull the coat, affect the dog's finished grooming and may develop into dandruff.

If the dog has short hair, he may be rinsed well and removed from the tub. If the dog is long-haired, rinse lightly and shampoo a second time. It takes two shampoos to get long hair properly clean. After the second sudsing, rinse every trace of shampoo out of the coat. Using warm water and the spray attachment, start at the head and ears and spray towards the tail and down the legs, rinsing until clear water comes off the dog, Photographs 64 and 65. If your dog was standing in the sudsy water, remember to pull the plug and let all the suds drain out of the tub before beginning the final rinse. Thoroughly rinsing is important. When soap is left in, the coat feels gritty, looks dull and is impossible to scissor or finish properly.

Toweling

Squeeze the excess water out of the coat. Cover the dog with a large, clean towel and carry him to the grooming table. Stand him up and blot the excess moisture from the coat with a towel, then let the dog shake if he wants to. Remove the cotton from the ears and use dry cotton to absorb any moisture inside the ear flaps.

Drying the Dog

Dry the dog with an electric hair dryer. As you begin drying, the dog will probably shiver because he is damp. The easiest way to keep him warm is to put him on a dry towel and let him curl his legs up under the body. The excess moisture will be absorbed by the towel while you dry the head, ears and body. If you brush a long-haired dog while he is drying, the coat will be fluffier and the dog will dry faster. Point the dryer at the area to be brushed and brush the hair in layers in the direction you want it to be in when the dog is dry. When the head, ears and body are dry, stand the dog on the grooming table. Brush and dry the legs and tail. The dog is now ready for final grooming work.

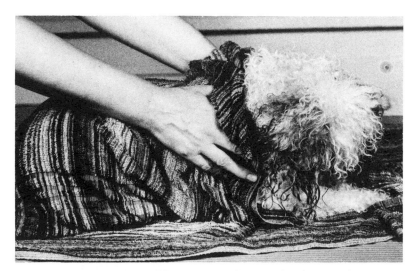

Photograph 66. Have a towel spread out on the grooming table before removing the dog from the tub. This towel will soak up excess moisture from the legs and underside while you towel his body.

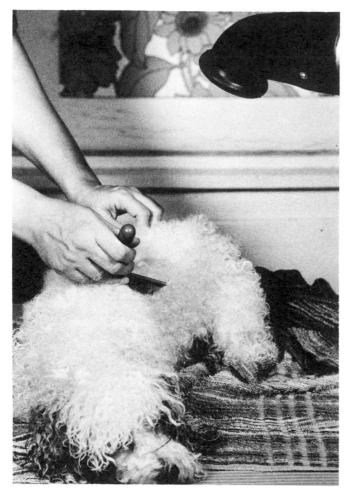

Photograph 67. Fluff drying can only be done with the use of an electric dryer. It gives a finish to a coat unobtainable by hand drying. It is done simply by directing a stream of warm air at a specific part of the coat while brushing it.

Bathing the Long Show Coat

The Maltese, Shih Tzu, Silky Terrier, Yorkshire Terrier, Lhasa Apso and Tibetan Terrier have long coats of various textures which fall flat over the sides of the body, hanging straight down to the ground in most instances. The Pekingese, Pomeranian, Bichon Frise, Papillon and Toy Spaniels have long coats of various textures. On any of these breeds, improper bathing can result in a loss of a show coat. Preparation for the bath requires a bit more work. Use a fine quality pin or bristle brush to remove all tangles from the long hair. Use the layering method described in the Brushing Chapter. Avoid using a comb to remove tangles from a show coat because it tends to tear out the hair. Break any mats apart with your fingers and try to lift them out with the brush. After the dog is completely brushed out, stand him on the grooming table. On the Maltese, Shih Tzu, Silky Terrier, Lhasa Apso, Yorkshire Terrier or Tibetan Terrier, use the brush to part the long show coat down the center of the back, letting the long hair fall to either side of the body. Bathe and rinse as instructed before, taking care to always keep the part down the center of the back to prevent coat damage and tangling on the long, flowing coated breeds. On all of the breeds mentioned in this section, when soaping the long hair, don't swirl the coat around with your fingers but do gently squeeze the shampoo through the coat, as if you were washing a delicate sweater. Shampoo twice and rinse thoroughly. On the long, flowing coated breeds, a creme rinse helps to make the hair hang straight. Take the dog out of the tub and blot with a towel. When using the towel, always blot the coat; do not rub the hair or you will cause tangling.

Drying this type of coat takes time, but it must be done in the proper manner with no short-cuts or you can ruin the hair. The dog should lie quietly on his side or stomach while being dried. The wet part, close to the grooming table top, should rest on a large, thick bath-size towel to keep the hair from tangling. The easiest way to dry the long hair is to part it in layers and brush lightly with the pin brush, as shown in Photograph 67, as the dryer blows on the coat. Keep layering the hair as described in the Brushing Chapter until one side is completely dry. Then pick up the dog, remove the wet towel from the table top, put down a dry towel and turn the dog over. Brush and dry the other side using the same layering method. Stand the dog on the grooming table. Lightly brush the hair once again to make it fall in the direction you want it to be when the dog is in the show ring.

Creme Rinse

Using a creme rinse on a long-haired dog after the bath is a matter of personal preference. On the long, flowing-coated breeds and the Papillon, Toy Spaniels and Bichon Frise, a creme rinse helps to make the hair more manageable and less inclined to mat after bathing. A creme rinse is not suggested for the Brussels Griffon, Pekingese or Pomeranian where a harsh outer coat is desirable.

Most of the companies mentioned in the shampoo section in this chapter also make creme rinses for dogs. If you wish to use a creme rinse, bathe the dog as instructed, rinse the shampoo from the hair, mix the creme rinse according to package directions, then pour over the hair. Squeeze the rinse through the coat with your fingers. Using clear water, rinse the hair lightly and dry as usual.

Bathing Tangled Dogs

There are several tangle removing preparations specially formulated for use on badly matted coats. When used according to directions, they make mat removal easier by saving many hours of brushing time. Tangle removing products work by penetrating the mats, coating the hair shaft with emollients which help to break the static lock, making the mats easier to remove. Three excellent products are made by Ring 5, Lambert Kay and Holiday. The Ring 5 product, Untangle, is a liquid and formulated to be used before bathing. The Lambert Kay product, No Tangle, is a liquid which may be used before or after the bath. The Holiday Detangle is an aerosol product and works best when used before the bath.

To remove tangles on dry hair before bathing, moisten all matted areas. Large tangled masses should be saturated to the skin. Depending on the dog's coat thickness, allow the product you use to remain on the hair at least fifteen minutes to help release the tangled lock, then brush the hair as usual. Both liquid products mentioned above may be left on the dog's coat until it dries and still be effective in helping to remove tangles.

While it is best to remove large tangled clumps before bathing, you can remove mats on wet hair after the bath with No Tangle. Shampoo with the appropriate shampoo and rinse thoroughly. Blot all the excess moisture from the dog's coat with a towel. Do not use a creme rinse. Holding the spray bottle of No Tangle about six inches away from the wet hair, moisten the entire coat. Large tangled masses should be saturated to the skin. Cover the dog with a towel to allow the No Tangle to penetrate the matted areas. After about ten minutes, begin brushing the hair dry as usual. Brush and dry the areas that are least matted first, allowing the detangler to remain as long as possible on the wet, heavily matted parts. If necessary, respray any stubborn tangled areas as you dry.

Dry Cleaning

Dry cleaning the dog's coat may be substituted for a shampoo and water bath when the dog is ill, in season, during the last weeks of pregnancy or immediately after puppies have been whelped. On certain breeds like the Pekingese or Pomeranian where a harshness is desired for the outer coat, bathing tends to soften and flatten this type of coat and these breeds are bathed only a few times a year. In between, the coat may be cleaned by using one of the following methods:

A. RING 5 WHITENER-CLEANER. This is a light powder in aerosol form. For complete penetration to the skin, fluff the hair with your fingers as you spray the powder into the coat. Brush out thoroughly. The product will not alter the dog's natural coat color.

B. DRI-BATH SHAMPOO. This is a quick and easy liquid shampoo which is applied with a sponge, washcloth or splashed directly from the squeeze bottle. Work the product into the soiled areas, towel all excess moisture and brush coat dry.

C. ONE CAN SILICONE DOG GROOMING POWDER, DISTILLED WATER and ONE TERRY WASHCLOTH. Place the dog on the grooming table or on the floor which has been covered with newspapers. Pour the distilled water into a bowl. Dip the washcloth into the water and wring it out. Wipe each back leg and foot, then use a towel to lightly dry each leg. Dip the washcloth into the water again and, taking one section at a time, do the same thing on the body, under the chest, the front of the chest, front legs and feet, neck and head. Lightly towel each section after you wipe over it. With the coat slightly damp, dust the silicone powder into the coat. Allow the hair to dry, then take a pin or bristle brush and remove all powder from the coat. Clean the nose with a dab of vaseline and check the eyes for any powder irritation. Use Eye-Brite to clean the eyes, if necessary.

D. ONE SPRAY BOTTLE OF COAT DRESSING FOR DOGS, ONE BOX POWDERED CORNSTARCH. Put the cornstarch in a metal powdered sugar shaker with handle (these can be purchased at the housewares counter of any variety store) for easy use. Spray the hair thoroughly with the Coat Dressing. Lightly towel dry the dog. Dust the cornstarch into the coat. Allow the hair to dry, then brush all traces of the cornstarch out of the coat. Clean nose and eyes as instructed in "C".

The Skin:
A Discussion and Description
of Common Problems

The most important factor in keeping any dog in prime condition comes from within. Nourishing food, plus the addition of vitamins and an internal skin and coat food supplement to the diet, will help keep your dog in top shape. Good skin health is important for all dogs, especially those to be shown in the breed ring. If the skin is not healthy, ultimately the hair will be affected. While the growth rate, texture and quality of coat is inherited, we enhance or destroy these by proper care or neglect. The condition of your dog's skin is one of the best indicators of his health. When the skin is soft, pink and well-toned (pinch or pull it up and it should immediately spring back), you can assume that your dog is in good condition.

A short or long-haired dog that is groomed regularly is less likely to suffer from skin disease. Regular brushing and combing distributes the natural oil throughout the coat and makes the skin clean and less susceptible to disease. Listed below are descriptions of common skin problems. Naturally, this book is about grooming and not meant to solve veterinary problems. However, this chapter is included because recognizing symptoms of skin trouble and taking immediate action may keep your dog healthier and happier and save you months of precious coat growing. Skin ailments are known to be among the most complicated and serious of canine problems.

Eczema or "Hot Spots"

Eczema or "Hot Spots" may be caused by parasites, insect bites, allergies, glandular failure, neglect in grooming or pre-disposition. While a dog does not inherit eczema or hot spots, certain strains seem to be more inclined to it than others. Affected areas may appear anywhere on the dog: at the base of the tail, on the back, in the area around the testicles, on the brisket under the front legs or on the neck and head.

Eczema is found in moist or dry form. With the moist type, the skin becomes red, scaly and itchy. A clear liquid starts oozing from the sores. The dog soon becomes so irritated that he bites and scratches the area, causing the infection to spread.

Eventually, the hair falls out. In many cases of grooming neglect, especially on the double-coated breeds, the affected areas start under clumps of matted hair.

Dry eczema starts with a dry, itchy area. The spot eventually becomes so irritated that the dog scratches persistently, breaking the skin and making it bleed.

If you notice hot spots or eczema, clip or pull out the hair around the sores. Whichever way you do it, the hair should come out easily. Then the dog should be completely brushed out and the hard-to-get spots under the front and back legs should be checked for rash. For temporary relief, apply Cortisynth cream or Ring 5 Medicated Spray to all affected areas. It is important that eczema be treated internally as well as externally, so a veterinarian should be consulted immediately. Once a correct diagnosis of the condition is made, treatment usually consists of injections followed by an oral medication and a special ointment for the sores.

Dry Skin or Dandruff

Two of the most common causes of dry skin and dandruff that can be corrected quickly are:

CAUSE: *Allowing the dog to sit close to the heat ducts during cold weather. After several months of constant dry heat, the skin becomes dry, and dandruff, similar to the human form, appears in the coat when the dog is brushed and seems impossible to get out.*

Suggestion: Lack of fat in a dog's diet is a major cause of dry skin in the winter. Try adding an internal skin and coat conditioner, a dietary supplement containing unsaturated fatty acid and vitamins, to your dog's diet. These products are formulated to correct dry skin dermatitis that causes itching and excessive scratching. It is an established fact that an animal's skin requires that it obtain unsaturated fatty acids in its diet. Many commercial dog foods and home prepared meals are low in these fats. Dry dog foods have most of the fat removed due to the fact the fat would become rancid if left in the feed. When fed daily, an internal skin and coat conditioner supplement helps to produce a luxurious coat and healthy, supple skin.

CAUSE: *Improper Bathing. This means not thoroughly pre-brushing a long-coated dog, using a harsh shampoo and not rinsing all the soap out of the coat.*

Suggestion: Before any long-coated dog is bathed, make sure the hair is thoroughly pre-brushed. When brushing, get down to the skin by making a part in the coat and letting your free hand separate the unbrushed hair from the section that is being brushed. By using this method, the brush bristles loosen and lift the dandruff. Bathe with a medicated shampoo. During the second shampoo, leave the lather on the hair for fifteen minutes before the final rinse. When rinsing, be sure all traces of soap and scurf are flushed out of the coat. If the hair is excessively dry, use a Balsam type human conditioner, applying it to the wet coat according to package directions.

Because dogs are more inactive during the hot weather and susceptible to gaining weight, there has been much discussion about summer diets and the discontinuation of vitamins or oil supplements. Do remember that hot weather, direct sunlight and warm winds also dry out the dog's coat just as they do human hair. It might be wise to continue the use of an internal skin and coat supplement in hot weather. There can be many other factors which cause dry skin and dandruff. If your dog scratches persistently at the skin, always consult a veterinarian.

Ringworm

Ringworm is a skin disease often confused with mange. Actually, Ringworm is not caused by a worm, but by an external fungus. The disease is called ringworm because infected areas take the form of a round or oval shape. Ringworm starts with small, scaly patches, usually on the head, which grow larger as the infection spreads.

At the onset of ringworm, the hair becomes coarse and brittle, eventually breaking off or falling out in stubby patches. If neglected, the disease spreads rapidly over the dog's body. Ringworm can be transmitted to humans so, if you suspect this disease, use a pair of rubber gloves to handle the dog. The dog should be taken to a veterinarian where proper diagnosis of the disease will be made by a Wood's Lamp or by culturing the fungus. Treatment consists of removing the hair from infected spots, cleaning the scabs to soften and loosen them and then applying a fungicidal preparation to dry the scabs. Treatment takes from several weeks to several months to cure, depending on how far advanced the disease was at the time of discovery. When treating your dog at home, remember to take any scaly matter or hair as it falls off the dog and burn it. Wash your hands with antibacterial soap before touching any parts of your body.

Acne

Acne is an irritation of the sebaceous glands which begins when the pores become clogged with dirt. Eventually, there is a bacteria build-up, resulting in pimples which may or may not discharge pus mixed with blood. The best way to control and cure simple acne is to flush out the sebaceous glands with a medicated shampoo to clean the pores of dirt and bacteria. Shampoo twice and during the second washing, leave the lather on the hair for about 15 minutes before beginning the final rinse. Then rinse well, making sure that all traces of soap and scurf are flushed out of the coat. Be sure to consult your veterinarian immediately if acne is suspected.

Fungus Infections

Fungus infections may be contacted from infected grassy or dirty areas. A scaly, itchy lesion often develops on areas where the hair is thin or in between the toes or pads under the feet. Temporarily, use a fungicidal spray, such as Ring 5 Medicated Spray, then contact your veterinarian immediately.

Contact Allergies

A dry rash may develop from direct contact with grass, bedding, wool rugs or certain chemicals used to disinfect grooming or kennel areas. Spray affected areas with Ring 5 Medicated Spray to stop the itching, then contact veterinarian immediately.

Scurf Patches

Dry, scaly patches may appear on the hindquarters, loin or head area of young puppies raised on a heating pad or under a heat lamp. Soften the patches by rubbing Cortisynth Cream or Vitamin A & D Ointment into the skin around the scabs several times a day. Spot bathe the patches with cotton and warm water, adding a tearless, mild shampoo if necessary. The patches will loosen and come off easily. After the patches are removed, keep the skin lubricated with baby oil or Vitamin A & D Ointment to prevent reoccurrence.

External Parasites and their Control

Fleas, lice, ticks and mites are the most common external parasites and all breeds of dogs can become infested by them at any time of the year. External parasites multiply rapidly and make a dog scratch persistently. When this happens on a long-haired breed, the dog pulls out his coat and leaves bald spots, in addition to damaging the skin. If the dog is neglected and allowed to become heavily infested with parasites, he may be stricken with some other serious illness because his physical condition has deteriorated.

If your dog has parasites, understanding their life cycle is important. Ridding the dog of parasites is only part of a somewhat unpleasant job. The other, and most important part is to prevent reinfestation and this can only be done by knowing how each organism undergoes the sequence of development from larvae to adult.

If you are a professional groomer, always isolate an infested dog until it has been attended to. Parasites spread quickly. Never cage an infested dog near other dogs in your shop to be groomed. When the infested dog has been treated, the cage should be thoroughly disinfected before putting another dog inside. Every piece of equipment used on the infested dog should be cleaned and disinfected before being used again.

Types of Parasites and their Cycles

FLEAS are tiny, brown, blood-sucking parasites. They bite the dog's skin causing an irritation. The dog tries to relieve this skin irritation by biting and scratching which often produces hot spots or a non-specific type of dermatitis. Fleas are picked up in damp, grassy or wooded areas and from direct contact with infested dogs. While they are easily seen on short-haired dogs, fleas can be difficult to spot on long-haired dogs because they bury themselves in the coat and move quickly about. Often, during a grooming session, you may notice small black specks in the coat. These specks are flea dirt on the dog's skin, made up mostly of blood sucked from the dog, passed through the flea's digestive system and eliminated as dried blood. Fleas produce large numbers of eggs which drop off the dog and get into floor cracks, rugs, under the furniture and in the dog's bedding.

The life cycle of the flea is as follows: eggs hatch in from two to twelve days, depending on the temperature, into maggot-like larvae. This larvae stage lasts from one to three weeks, depending on temperature and moisture. Next, they spin small

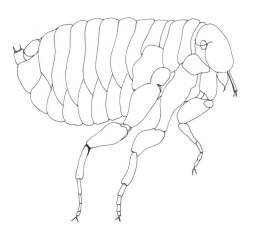

Diagram 2. The infamous flea. This bane of the canine has pestered dogs and their owners for centuries. While, today there are many effective flea control agents available, diligent measures must still be used to eradicate these stubborn parasites.

Diagram 3. Fleas live on the blood of the host dog, extracted from the body as shown. If an infestation is left unchecked, the fleas can multiply enough to cause the host anemia and worse.

cocoons and remain in this stage for about two weeks, then hatch into adults. These new fleas look for something to feed on and eventually reinfest the dog. Fleas are the intermediate host for tapeworm eggs.

To control fleas, both the animal and its environment must be treated. To kill fleas on the dog, select one of the following methods:

A. Aerosol Flea Spray or Flea Powder. When using an aerosol insecticide, be sure to read label directions carefully before applying the product to the skin and hair. When dusting with a powder, work it into the skin for maximum effectiveness.

B. Parasite Shampoo. There are special oil-base insecticidal shampoos designed specifically to rid the dog of parasites. The killing agent in most of these products is Pyrethrins, a non-toxic pesticide which is highly effective and safe for use on animals. Before using an insecticidal shampoo, place a drop or two of mineral oil into each eye and coat the genitals with vaseline. Follow instructions in the Bathing Chapter, massaging the shampoo into the hair until the entire body is covered. Allow the lather to remain on the coat for about ten minutes for the insecticide to take full effect, then rinse thoroughly and dry as usual.

C. Flea Dip. These come in package and bottle form and are mixed with water according to package instructions. The best time to dip a long-haired dog is immediately after a bath. Follow instructions for bathing, using your regular shampoo. After the final rinse, take the dog out of the tub and towel the excess moisture from the coat. Prepare the dip. Put the dog back into the tub. Using a plastic cup, start at the neck and pour the mixture down the back and over the sides of the body and legs. Keep pouring the solution over the dog until all areas of the body are saturated. Don't forget the hard-to-get areas under the ears, down the chest and between the front and back legs. When working above the eyes, place your free hand over them and tilt the head upward and backward to make the dip roll down the back of the neck and not into the eyes. Use a washcloth to put dip on the face. Do not rinse the hair after the dip is applied. Remove the dog from the tub and dry as usual.

To keep the dog from becoming reinfested, clean all the areas in your home where your pet spends a lot of time. Vacuum the bedding, rugs and furniture. Be sure to clean the cracks in the floor and around the baseboards. There are many spray and powder insecticides which can be used but with great care. Stubborn cases may have to be turned over to a pest control expert who possesses both the know-how and proper insecticides.

As an added protection, flea collars and tags have been effective in controlling parasites. The flea collars are available at most pet shops and are guaranteed effective for three months. Once placed around the dog's neck, the collar starts killing fleas instantly. For best results when using a flea collar, put it on loosely, cut off any excess collar and keep the dog dry while the collar is worn. Flea tags are discs which can be attached easily to the dog's regular collar. They are also guaranteed effective for three months. Certain breeds occasionally experience sensitivity reactions to a flea collar. If this happens to your dog, remove the collar immediately and switch to the flea tag.

LICE are small grey parasites which are spread from direct contact with an infested dog. Two types of lice infest the dog, the biting louse and the sucking louse. Both types are difficult to see on a long-haired dog because they are so small. Lice do not move around on the dog's body, but burrow into one place (usually under the ears and on the back of the neck) and remain there sucking the dog's blood. If neglected, the dog's condition deteriorates and he becomes susceptible to anemia. Lice spend their entire life cycle on the dog. The female produces large numbers of eggs which hatch in about one week. These eggs, or "nits," are light colored shafts that attach themselves to the dog's hair and become adult lice in about three weeks. The easiest way to rid a dog of lice is to clip off all the hair (be sure to burn it once it's off the dog) and give the dog a parasite shampoo or dip. Even though lice spend their entire cycle on the dog's body, the bedding should be disinfected. It is possible that some eggs could get into the bed through the shedding of coat.

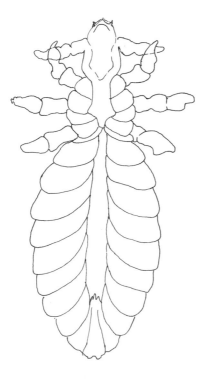 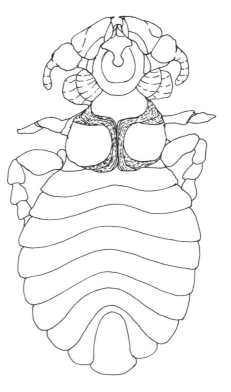

Diagram 4. The Sucking Louse   Diagram 5. The Biting Louse

TICKS come in many different varieties. There are three major tick species in the United States:

1. Rocky Mountain Spotted Fever Tick

2. American Dog Tick
Reddish-brown in color, turning a slate gray after feeding. Males have white perpendicular lines on backs and females have shield-like white markings on back.

3. Brown Dog Tick
Most common variety. Males are reddish-brown. Females are taupe color. Males and females have no white markings.

Brown dog ticks are found in every climate, but are most prevalent in damp wooded areas, sandy beaches and places where infested dogs have been housed. They attach themselves to the dog's skin and feed on his blood to reproduce. The male tick is small and reddish-brown. He does not feed and does not increase in size. The female tick is a taupe or slate color. She does feed and enlarges up to ten times her normal size as she gorges. Mating occurs while the female feeds on the dog. Once the female has her fill of the dog's blood (at this stage, she is usually the size of a kidney bean), she drops off and hunts a place to lay her eggs. In the house, this place is usually under the furniture or drapes, in the carpets or baseboards. The tick never lays its eggs on the animal. The female brown dog tick lays several thousand eggs, which hatch into larvae, or seed ticks, in three to eight weeks. After hatching, these seed

Diagram 6. The Brown Dog Tick (male)

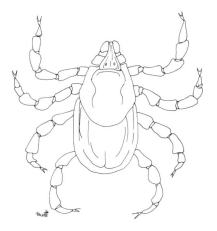

Diagram 7. The Brown Dog Tick (female)

Diagram 8. The tick feeds by piercing the dog's skin with its tiny, barbed teeth and sucking the host's blood. It also secretes saliva into the dog's body which can cause various diseases.

ticks hide away and molt to become nymphs. The nymphs, in turn, molt into adult ticks and the life cycle is complete. New ticks look for a dog to feed on, but they can live in the house up to two years without attaching themselves to a dog.

If you do not follow the proper procedure to rid the dog and house of ticks, the dog will become constantly reinfested and his physical condition will deteriorate. Follow these steps to remove ticks:

1. Examine the dog and locate all ticks. Check all small lumps on the skin; they may be ticks. Check inside the ears. Check between the toes and foot pads. When a dog becomes infested outdoors, ticks usually attach themselves to the feet.
2. Soak all visible ticks with alcohol. Alcohol helps paralyze and asphyxiate the tick, causing it to loosen the head which is attached to the dog.
3. Use tweezers to gently pull the entire tick from the dog. Do not leave the tick's head buried in the skin. This may cause infection.
4. Swab the skin with white iodine or merthiolate when the tick is pulled out.
5. Destroy the ticks taken from the dog.
6. Shampoo or dip the dog following instructions under FLEAS.
7. Disinfect the dog's bedding and spray baseboards, carpets, etc. near the bed with a non-toxic insecticide. Stubborn cases of tick infestation may have to be turned over to a pest control expert.

THE DEMODECTIC MANGE MITE, also called the Follicular Mange mite or Red Mange mite, is a tiny cigar-shaped creature which causes Demodectic Mange. Symptoms of the disease are loss of hair (especially on the forehead, cheeks, under the eyes and on the body near the front legs) and a thickening of the skin. Two classifications of lesions develop in Demodectic Mange—*Squamous,* the milder type, where there is some loss of hair and a slightly reddened skin, and *Pustular,* the more serious type, where pustules appear, oozing pus and blood from the infected areas, and the skin becomes very thick and red.

Demodectic Mange mites live in the hair follicles and sebaceous glands, which causes the hair to fall out on the infected animal. The entire life cycle of this mite is not known, but after the eggs hatch, the larvae mature into adult mites quickly and reproduce rapidly.

When Demodectic Mange is suspected, the dog should be taken to a veterinarian who will take a skin scraping to determine the presence of mites. The veterinarian will prescribe a treatment, which must be followed exactly as directed, since Demodectic Mange is one of the most difficult diseases to cure. Treatment may consist of injections or medication which will destroy the mange mites through the bloodstream. If Demodectic Mange is noticed and treated immediately, it can be arrested in a short time but, if neglected, the dog may suffer many months before being cured.

THE SARCOPTIC MANGE MITE causes a disease called Sarcoptic Mange or Scabies. Under a microscope, this type of mite appears round, with many pairs of short legs. The Sarcoptic Mange mite causes intense itching as it tunnels into the dog's skin. The skin becomes dry and thick and a small scale formation develops. This formation increases rapidly and soon crusts form. Spots are usually first noticed around the head area but they can quickly spread over the entire body.

The life cycle of the Sarcoptic Mange mite is about two weeks. After the female tunnels into the dog's skin, she lays eggs which hatch into larvae in a few days. The larvae molt into nymphs, then molt again into adults. Just one female can produce

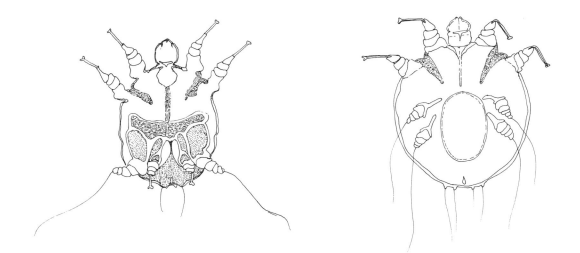

Diagram 9. The Sarcoptic Mange Mite (male, left; female, right)

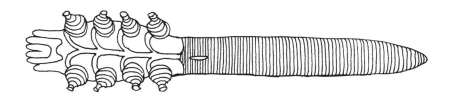

Diagram 10. The Demodectic Mange Mite

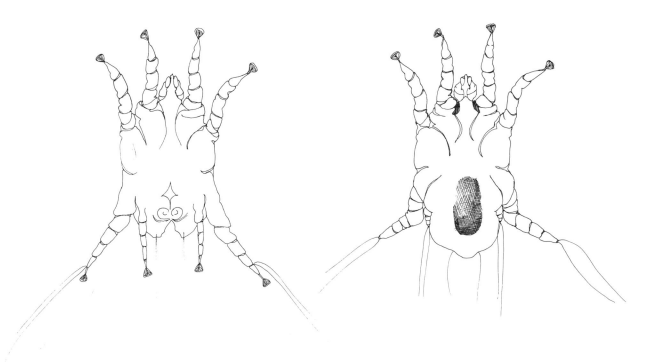

Diagram 11. The Ear Mange Mite (male, left; female, right)

hundreds of thousands of mites in a few months. The female is the only Sarcoptic Mange mite to burrow into the skin. Males and nymphs live on the surface of the skin underneath the mange scabs.

Sarcoptic Mange spreads rapidly and this type of mange can spread to humans. Diagnosis must be made by a veterinarian, who will take skin scrapings to determine the presence of the Sarcoptic mites.

EAR MITES are common in dogs. The *Otodectes cynotis,* or ear mite is picked up by direct contact with an infested dog and completes its entire life cycle in the dog's ear. Usually, these mites are not visible to the naked eye, but easily suspected when the dog shakes its head in a violent manner or constantly scratches its ears. There is also the presence of brownish fragments inside the ear, a combination of dried blood, wax and excretions from the ear itself. It is best to let a veterinarian give the first treatment, which involves removal of the fragments and application of an oily solution containing an insecticide. Then, if the treatment is continued at home, the condition will clear up rapidly. Remember, if you do not follow your veterinarian's advice for home treatment, any mites on the hair around the ears can crawl back into the ear and reinfest the dog.

Clipper Burn

Clipper burn is a painful sore or rash which sometimes inflames the sensitive areas (face, throat, underside of tail and genitals) of dogs after clipping. Many dogs suffer from clipper burn every time they are clipped, while others are never bothered.

Clipper burn progresses like a chain reaction. First, the skin becomes red and irritated, then the dog starts scratching. If the irritated areas are ignored and not treated at this stage, the animal continues to scratch until the tender areas are raw with painful, open sores. Many times, these open sores become so infected that the skin is permanently scarred and the hair never grows back.

To prevent clipper burn on a sensitive dog:

1. Don't use a fine blade on a young dog or one that you have never clipped before. Remember, you can always take more hair off, but you can't put it back.

2. If you know the dog is sensitive to the clipper blade, do not rough-cut the delicate areas before shampooing. Instead, brush out the dog, rough-cut the safe areas, then bathe the dog using a medicated shampoo, which will help to control clipper burn.

3. When clipping sensitive parts after the dog has been shampooed and dried, be sure the clipper blade is clean and cool. Never use a warm blade to clip a sensitive dog. If necessary, use one of the aerosol blade coolers to prevent the blade from getting hot.

4. When clipping the sensitive areas, always hold the clipper blade FLAT against the skin. Do not (even slightly) point the blade edges into the skin. This seems to be the primary reason for clipper rash on the genital area of male dogs. Clipping underneath the back legs is an awkward job and, if the groomer holds the clippers at a slight angle instead of flat against the skin, it could cause enough irritation to start the dog scratching.

5. Do not use a dull blade or one with missing teeth to clip the sensitive areas.

6. When the dog's nails are cut, smooth the rough edges of each nail immediately with a file or emery board. One reason why clipper burn is a problem on a Poodle's face is because the dog can scratch that part easily. Think of the irritation that rough nail edges could cause!

7. After the dog is clipped, use Cortisynth cream, Ring 5 Medicated Spray, Bactine or Seabreeze on the delicate areas to prevent irritation. The product you use at this stage should be greaseless, so the dog will not try to rub it off.

8. Advanced cases of clipper rash (open sores or scabs) will require an antibiotic ointment which must be prescribed by a veterinarian.

Assuming you have carefully observed all of the above steps and your dog still clipper burns, ask your veterinarian about the use of antihistamines.

Wrapping the Show Coat

The Maltese, Shih Tzu, Yorkshire Terrier, Lhasa Apso and other long-haired breeds with coats hanging flat over the sides of the body and touching the ground, often experience hair breakage from a variety of causes, such as static electricity from carpets, damage to hair ends by gravel in kennel runs, etc. For show purposes, adult coats on these breeds should be long and flowing. To encourage growth, prevent split ends and coat loss, the body hair and head furnishings may be oiled and wrapped as instructed below.

You will need the following supplies:

1. Coat Oil. This should be a light oil in aerosol form, such as Ring 5 Bright & Shine, St. Aubrey Coatasheen or Coat Oil.
2. Wrapping Materials. Choose one of the following:
   A. Handi-Wipes
   B. Waxed Paper
   C. Polyethlene Bags (The type sold in markets for trash) or Baggies
   D. Florists' or Tissue Paper
   E. Marcel Interfold Dry Waxed Paper (available at Bakery Shops)
   F. Nylon Tulle (*not* Nylon Net)
   G. Silk Material

   These seven suggestions are not meant to confuse the reader. Because of the many kinds of coat textures, climates and humidity, the hair will respond differently to the above materials. Experiment a bit and find out which is best for your breed.

   Cut whichever material you choose into oblong strips, each from 3 to 4 inches wide. The length of each strip varies according to the dog's coat. Cut each one at least 2 inches longer than the hair you want to wrap. Be sure to cut enough strips. You will need at least 22 to do a complete wrapping.
3. Small Latex Bands. These may be purchased at your local dental supply company or mail ordered from Show Dog Products, P. O. Box 7952, Long Beach, California 90807.

Instructions For Wrapping the Coat

Photograph 68. Breeds which require wrapping usually are groomed with a center part in the back. Then the long hair is parted in 2″ to 3″ sections downward from the center part. Stand the dog on the grooming table with hindquarters facing you and begin at the base of the skull, parting the hair lengthwise down the back to the tail.

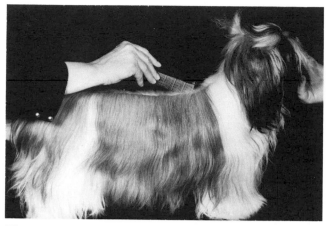

Photograph 68. Straightening the center part in preparation for wrapping.

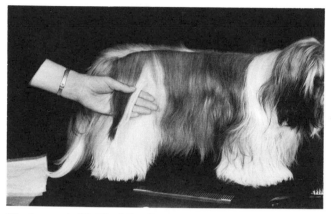

Photograph 69. Start the first wrapping over the hind leg.

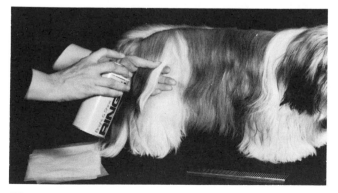

Photograph 70. Spray a light oil on the hair section before wrapping.

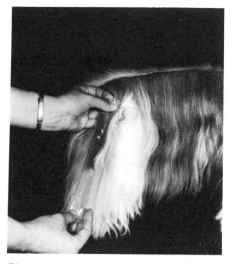

Photograph 71. The wrapping material is folded in thirds around the hair.

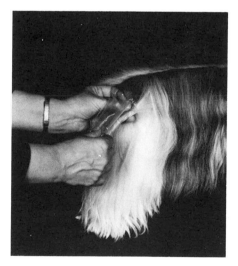

Photograph 72. After folding the wrapping in thirds, fold in half toward the dog's body.

Photograph 69. Start at the center part at the hindquarters near the tail and part the hair downward. Now make another part downward near the front of the back leg. This section of hair will be your first wrapping.

Photograph 70. Lightly oil this section of hair. Place one oblong wrapping strip behind the hair section and fold 1/3 of the strip over lengthwise.

Photograph 71. Fold the remaining third of the strip over lengthwise. (Be sure the strip is long enough to cover the ends of the hair.)

Photograph 72. Fold the wrapping in half upward towards the body.

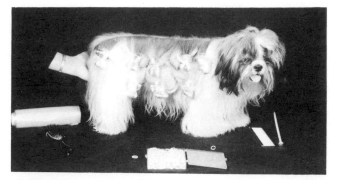

Photograph 75. Here one side of the Shih Tzu model is parted and wrapped. Also shown are the various tools and supplies needed to wrap up a coat. For very heavy coats, two rows of wrappings are preferred to one.

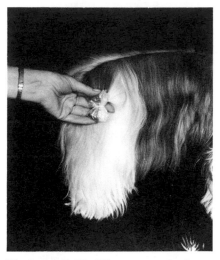

Photograph 73. When properly done, a finished wrapping should look like this.

Photograph 76. The number of wrappings on the chest depend on the amount of the coat.

Photograph 74. The hair over the loin is wrapped in the second wrapping.

Photograph 77. Two wrappings secure the hair below the anus.

Photograph 73. Fold in half once again and fasten with a latex band. Use a band small enough to turn only twice.

Photograph 74. Work forward, making your next part over the loin. Oil and wrap this section of hair.

Photograph 75. Keep working forward, parting the hair in 2″ or 3″ sections, then oiling and wrapping. This photograph shows one side parted and wrapped.

Photograph 76. When you reach the front of the chest, turn the dog around to stand facing you. The hair can be parted and wrapped into two or three sections, depending on the amount of coat.

Photograph 78. Make one wrapping of the *hair* at the end of the tail. Never wrap any part of the dog's tail bone.

Photograph 79. Head furnishings must be wrapped to promote growth and retard staining, but the dog's well-being should be considered when wrapping this part of the coat.

Photograph 80. The second facial wrapping.

73

Photograph 81. Depending on the amount of coat present, make one or two wrappings for the beard.

Photograph 82. Wrapping the feathering at the ends of the ears protects them from damage. As with the tail, wrap only the hair. If any part of the leather is accidentally wrapped, serious damage could result.

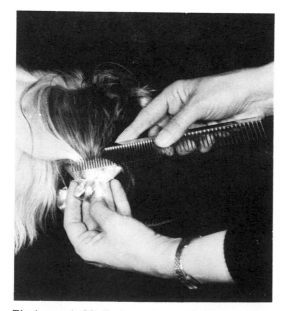

Photograph 83. To be sure you have wrapped only the hair of the ears, insert your comb above the wrapping. If the teeth pass through easily, you've made a good wrapping. If not, you must rewrap.

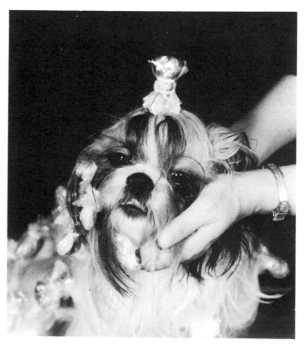

Photograph 84. The wrapped topknot.

Photograph 77. Wrap the opposite side of the dog the same way. Then turn the dog to stand with hindquarters facing you. Part the hair below the anus in half and make two wrappings as shown.

Photograph 78. Depending on the breed, brush out and oil the tail feathering. Make one wrapping at the end of the tail. Be sure the latex band encircles the hair only and not the end of the tail.

Photograph 79. The head furnishings are also wrapped to prevent staining and hair breakage. Begin by parting the hair from the inside corner of the eye to the edge of the mouth as shown. Oil the hair. Place a wrapper under the hair, then fold and fasten as previously instructed. *Caution: Before wrapping, be sure that this section of hair is separated from any beard hair under the chin. Never wrap top and bottom hair together or the dog will not be able to open his mouth.*

Photograph 80. The second facial wrapping is made by parting the hair downward from in front of the ear. Wrap and fasten this section as previously instructed, taking care not to get any of the ear into the wrapping. Wrap the opposite side of the face.

Photograph 81. Shows the hair under the chin fastened in one wrapping. If there is abundant beard hair, use two wrappings instead of one.

Photograph 82. If the dog has hanging ears with long feathering, this hair may be wrapped. Fold the wrapping around the feathering, making sure that it is below the ear leather. Fold lengthwise in thirds, then fold in half twice and fasten with a latex band.

Photograph 83. When both ears are wrapped, take a comb and see if you can place the teeth between the wrappings and the ear leathers. Never wrap any part of the ear leather. If you do, circulation will stop and the ear will be damaged.

Photograph 84. The topknot may also be wrapped. Part the hair from the outside corner of each eye upward to the inside corner of each ear. Then part the hair straight across the top of the head, from ear to ear. Oil and fasten this section with one wrapper and a latex band.

If the dog tries to chew out the wrappings, spray a little Bitter Apple or Capsicum (liquid pepper) onto the wrappings to discourage him.

Take down the wrappings about twice a week. Unwrap one section and brush out the hair. Then unwrap the next section and brush out, etc., until one complete side is taken down. Turn the dog around and do the other side. If there is a ring or matted area where the band encircled the wrapping, spray it with oil and gently pull the hair apart with your fingers before brushing. It should take about 45 minutes to one hour to unwrap, brush and rewrap the dog's coat.

The Affenpinscher

The Affenpinscher or Monkey Dog, as the breed was often called in Europe, is a plucky, vivacious and intelligent little dog. Although it is a member of the Toy Group, the Affenpinscher is spirited and terrier-like in attitude and demeanor.

Description of Coat

The Breed Standard describes the coat as "an important factor. It is short and dense in certain parts and shaggy and longer in others, but should be hard and wiry. It is longer and more loose and shaggy on the legs and around the eyes, nose and chin, giving the typical monkey-like appearance from whence comes his name. The best color is black, matching his eyes and fiery temperament. However, black with tan markings, red, gray and other mixtures are permissible. Very light colors and white markings are a fault."

Brushing and Combing

The coat should be brushed about 2 to 3 times each week. Use a firm natural bristle brush or palm brush. Before brushing, spray the hair with an aerosol protein conditioner or coat dressing. Brush first against the growth of hair, from the tail to the head, to loosen as much dead hair and skin flaking as possible. Then brush in the opposite direction, from head to tail, and down the legs. Brush the facial hair carefully. After brushing, comb through the coat, using a medium-tooth comb, to be sure all dead hair and tangles are removed.

Bathing

If the coat is brushed properly about three times a week, the Affenpinscher will rarely need a bath. On show dogs, bathing is done rarely, as shampooing softens the coat. If a shampoo is necessary for a show dog, always bathe at least 10 days before exhibition to allow the harsh texture to return to the hair. For both pets and show dogs, when a bath is necessary, follow shampoo directions found in the Bathing Chapter. Use a texturizer or protein shampoo, bathe twice, then rinse well. Do not use a creme rinse. Follow directions for drying found in the Bathing Chapter.

Grooming the Affenpinscher

There is some controversy as to how much grooming should be done on an Affenpinscher. Most experts agree, however, that the hard coat should be trimmed and tidied just enough to preserve the characteristic rough appearance.

The trimming work on the body may be done by plucking, stripping or clipping. Use whichever method is best suited to your grooming schedule. For correct plucking and stripping techniques, please refer to the Brussels Griffon Chapter. If you wish to clip the Affenpinscher, use an Oster Clipper with a #4 or #5 blade.

Trimming the Body and Neck

It seems more comfortable and acceptable to the dog to begin trimming behind the ears and work backwards to the tail, leaving the head to be done last. By plucking, stripping or clipping with a #4 or #5 blade, shorten the hair on the back and sides of the neck and under the throat. Then work from the shoulders to the tail and trim the body, making the back appear straight. The hair length should be about 3/4 of an inch long on the top and sides of the body, then blend into slightly longer hair on the brisket and chest. Do not leave too much hair on the brisket as this tends to make the dog appear long and low when the opposite effect is desired. However, do not take off too much hair and make the Affenpinscher look too delicate and without substance.

Trimming the Shoulders, Hindquarters, Front and Back Legs

Trim from the shoulders downward to the elbow. At the place where the front legs join the body, be careful to remove all straggly hairs and blend the body hair well into the leg hair to keep the dog from appearing "out" at the elbows.

The hair on the hindquarters and under the tail should be trimmed to create a short-bodied, compact appearance. As you did at the shoulders, be sure to blend the body hair well into the hair on the back legs.

Pluck only the straggly hairs from the front and back legs, leaving the feathering loose and shaggy. When trimming the forelegs, they should appear straight when viewed from any angle.

Trimming the Tail

Pluck, strip or clip the hair on all sides of the tail stump

Trimming the Feet

Scissor the hair from between the pads underneath each foot. Then place each foot down in a normal standing position and scissor around the paw to make it appear round and compact looking.

Trimming the Stomach

On pet Affenpinscher, you may clip the stomach with a #10 blade. Be sure to clip only the stomach hair, taking care not to trim too far up under the chest.

Trimming the Ears

The Affenpinscher's ears should appear sleek, erect and high-set. Using clippers with a #10 blade, hold the ear flat and clip from the base to the top on the outside of each ear. Carefully clip the inside of each ear in the same direction. (Many exhibitors prefer to clip only 3/4 of the ear instead of the entire ear.) Then scissor carefully around the edges of each ear to remove all straggly hairs and emphasize the point at the top.

The Eyes

The Affenpinscher's eyes are large and round and require daily care. Refer to the Eye Care Chapter for instructions. The eyes can be irritated easily by wisps of long hairs touching the eyeball. To prevent this from happening, shorten the hairs at the inside corner of the eyes by plucking with your thumb and finger. Do not overpluck. Shorten the hair just enough to keep any long ends from falling into the eyes. *Do not cut this hair with scissors.*

Trimming the Head

Correct trimming is necessary to achieve the Affenpinscher's proper expression. The dense, wiry facial hair should stand out all around the head. Comb the hair on the top of the head upward and pluck or scissor to a length of about 1/2 inch, emphasizing a well-domed forehead. Comb the eyebrows upward and forward and trim to the same length. The eyebrows should appear bushy, but must not hang down over the eyes. Trimming the eyebrows correctly, along with plucking the wispy hairs between the eyes as instructed before, opens the eye area and creates a pleasant expression. The hair on the sides of the face, in back of the outside edge of the eyes, is trimmed short to blend with the neck hair. Comb the beard and moustache outward. The beard should appear profuse; and scissoring should be done only to remove straggly hairs. When finished, the eyebrows, hair on the cheeks and beard blend together to create the monkey-look as described in the Standard.

Photograph 85 shows the finished Affenpinscher

Photograph 85. The Affenpinscher is a German breed that was originally used as a ratter and stable dog. Even today, far removed from his traditional work, he is still a self-assured, brave little dog. He should be groomed to appear neat, but should never look over-trimmed.

The Bichon Frise

The Bichon Frise (pronounced *Bee-shon Free-zay*) is a relatively new breed to the United States. Before grooming a Bichon, it is important to know what a good specimen of the breed looks like, so for those not familiar with this delightful breed, a description follows.

The Standard of the breed states that the Bichon Frise is a sturdy, lively dog of stable temperament with a stylish gait and an air of dignity and intelligence. The Bichon is solid white or can be white with cream, apricot or grey on the ears and/or body. The height at the withers should not exceed 12 inches and not be under eight inches. The body is slightly longer than it is tall, well developed with good spring of ribs. The back inclines gradually from the withers to a slight rise over the loin, which is large and muscular. Legs and feet are strong boned. The front should appear straight. Hindquarters should be well angulated. The feet resemble cat's paws and are tight and round. The Bichon has a tail covered with long, flowing hair which is carried gaily and curved to lie over the back. The head should be in proportion to the size of the dog. The skull is broad and somewhat round, but not coarse. Eyes are black or dark brown with black rims, and they are large, round, expressive and alert. Lips and nose should be black. Ears are dropped and covered with long, flowing hair. The ear leather should reach approximately halfway to the muzzle. The coat is profuse, silky and loosely curled. There is an undercoat. For show purposes, the standard calls for a minimum of two inches of hair. For pets, the coat may be any length, depending on personal preference and climate.

The Bichon is groomed to look as natural as possible. There is no clipping. Some scissoring is required, however, to achieve the full, rounded, "powder puff" effect called for in the Standard, but there must never be an exaggerated plush scissored look to the Bichon.

Brushing and Combing

Because the Bichon's hair is long and almost non-shedding, regular brushing and coat care, at least three times a week, is a most important part of grooming. Before each brushing, spray the hair with an aerosol protein conditioner or coat dressing to moisten the coat. On the shorter pet and puppy coats, use a slicker brush, following

Photograph 86. The Bichon Frise is a new breed to the American scene and dog lovers have been quick to take notice of him. Small size, attractive appearance and a pleasant personality are all plus factors that have helped the Bichon make many new friends in a short time. His beautiful coat does require regular trimming and grooming, though, to look its best. *Missy Yuhl*

directions in the Brushing Chapter. To be sure you are brushing to the skin, part the hair as you brush, letting your free hand separate the unbrushed hair from the section being brushed.

For the longer show coats, use a pin or natural bristle brush. The longer hair is best brushed by layering the hair. Instructions for layer brushing are found in the Brushing Chapter. On the long coated show Bichons, it is permissible to use a slicker brush on the bottoms of the legs and feet.

After the coat has been brushed thoroughly, use the half-fine, half-medium comb to go through the hair once again to be sure all tangles have been removed.

Pre-Bath Preparations

Clean ears, cut nails and check anal glands.

Bathing and Drying

Follow instructions in the Bathing Chapter, using a whitener shampoo for the body, legs, tail, ears and parts of the head area. Always use a tearless shampoo when working near the eyes. Give two shampoos, rinse well and follow with a creme rinse.

Brush the hair dry as instructed in the Bathing Chapter. When drying the coat, brush with light strokes that lift the hair, rather than flatten it, to achieve the "powder puff" effect called for in the Standard.

Finishing the Bichon Frise

THE STOMACH: This step is optional and a matter of personal preference. Many Bichon owners use clippers around the genital area to keep the hair from staining. If you own a male dog and excessive hair staining becomes a problem, clip this area with a #10 blade. Holding up the front legs with your free hand, as shown in Photograph 87, point clippers upward, start just above the genitals and clip off the excess hair.

THE TAIL: Comb the hair on the tail. The Bichon should have a profuse looking tail with no scissoring being necessary.

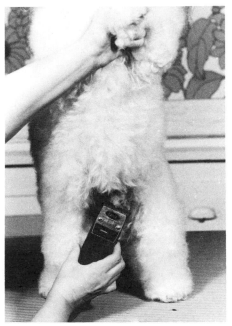

Photograph 87. Clipping the stomach area of a Bichon is a matter personal preference. Some male dogs will have an excessive amount of urine stains in the area if they are not clipped. When clipping the hair on the penis, always go with the grain of the hair.

81

BACK FEET AND LEGS: Stand the dog on the grooming table with the hindquarters facing you. Begin working on the back feet. Holding one foot in your hand, use scissors to clean out the hair between the pads on the underside of the foot. Place the foot back on the table in a normal standing position and use scissors to trim around the paw, as shown in Photograph 88, to achieve the "cat's paw" look called for in the breed standard. Do not scissor closely around the toes. The foot should appear wide and in balance with the rest of the leg, as shown in Photograph 89.

Comb the hair on the back leg up and out to fluff the coat. Use scissors to tip the coat and remove any untidy hairs, shaping the leg to appear round and solid, almost cylindrical in appearance. The easiest way to shape the leg is to begin at the foot and work up to the hips. When one part of the leg is shaped, begin again at the foot and scissor another part up to the hips, as shown in Photograph 90. Work completely around the leg in this manner, holding the scissors flat against the hair you are working on. When scissoring near the hock at the back of the leg, emphasize any angulation the dog may have, as shown in Photograph 91. Hold up the tail with your free hand. Use scissors to shape the area under the tail round, as shown in Photograph 92. Continue working up to the hindquarters, shaping the hair round. Scissor the opposite back leg and foot. Be sure the hair on both legs is scissored to the same length.

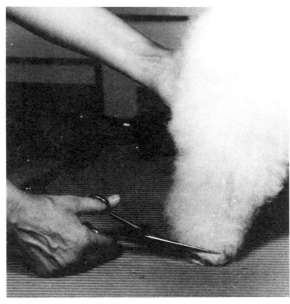

Photograph 88. In trimming the hind feet you are trying to achieve both a compact look and an overall impression of width. If you hold the foot up that you are not trimming, the dog will not be able to fidget with the foot you will be working on.

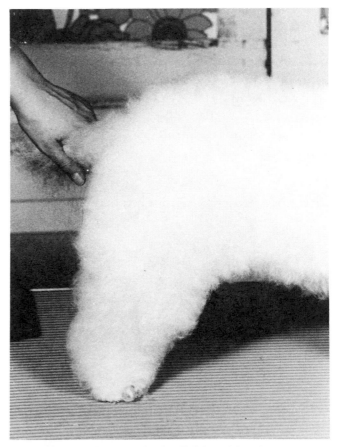

Photograph 89. Here is the finished hind foot as it should properly appear.

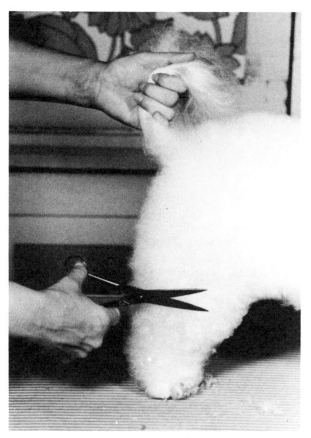

Photograph 90. To trim the outside of the hindlegs lay the scissor flat against the leg and ''tip'' the hairs. In the Bichon the desired impression is one of roundness and softness overall.

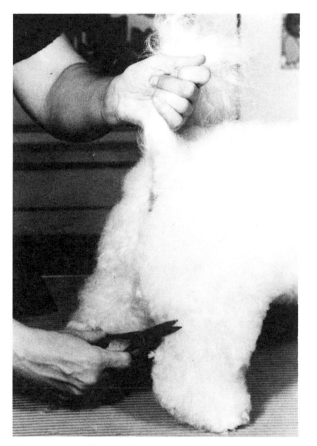

Photograph 92. Continue up to the hindquarters, working ''in the round.'' In the area around and under the tail proper trimming enhances a good tail-set and improves a weak one.

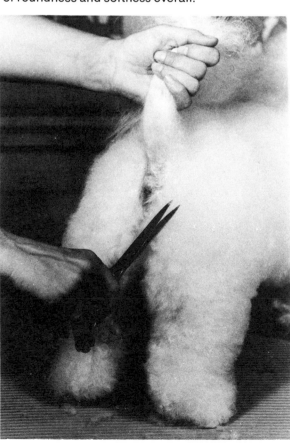

Photograph 91. Careful trimming on the back of the hindleg above the hock joint will enhance the Bichon's rear angulation.

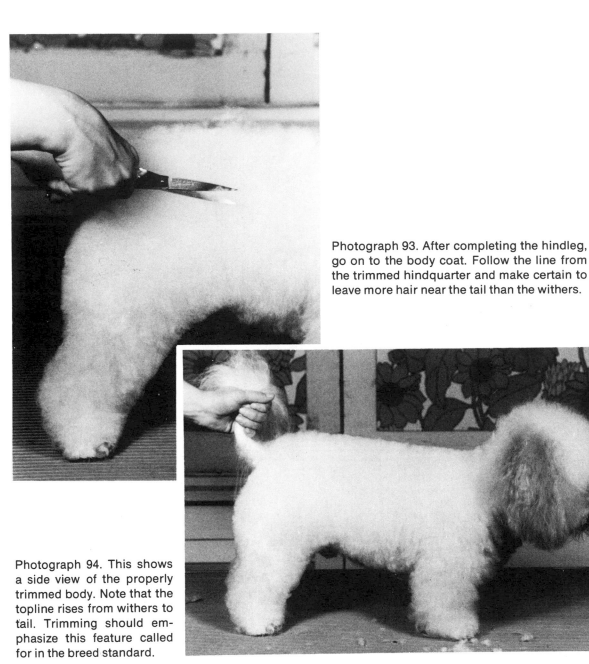

Photograph 93. After completing the hindleg, go on to the body coat. Follow the line from the trimmed hindquarter and make certain to leave more hair near the tail than the withers.

Photograph 94. This shows a side view of the properly trimmed body. Note that the topline rises from withers to tail. Trimming should emphasize this feature called for in the breed standard.

THE BODY: Comb the body hair upward and outward to fluff the coat away from the body. Continue working forward from the hindquarters, as shown in Photograph 93, scissoring the hair on the body to follow the natural, round contours of the dog. Do remember that the Standard calls for a gradual rise from the withers up over the loin to the tail and, when scissoring the topline, you must emphasize this gradual slope, as shown in Photograph 94. The Standard calls for a minmum of two inches of hair for a show coat, so do not scissor off too much hair. Just remove enough hair to achieve the full, rounded effect called for in the Standard. If the dog is a pet, the hair can be scissored much shorter for easier maintenance.

NECK, SHOULDERS AND FRONT OF CHEST: Comb the hair on the back of the neck up and out. Scissor this hair slightly shorter than the body, in a gradual blending from the shoulders up to the skull, as shown in Photograph 95. Turn the dog around to

Photograph 95. The hair on the neck and shoulder should be trimmed slightly shorter than the body coat. It must be gradually blended into the body coat to create a smooth look.

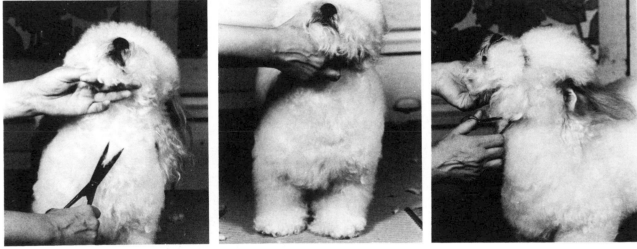

Photograph 96. The hair on the neck is trimmed slightly shorter than surrounding areas of coat.

Photograph 97. As you trim closer to the forelegs, graduate the coat to make it slightly longer than the hair on the throat.

Photograph 98. Use thinning shears under the ears if there is too much hair there. Be sure to keep the thinning shears close to the skin in this.

stand facing you. Hold up the head with your free hand and shorten the hair on the throat, as shown in Photograph 96. As you scissor down the front of the chest, the hair becomes slightly longer, as shown in Photograph 97, and is combed downward after scissoring. If the hair under the ears appears thick and clumpy, use thinning shears, as shown in Photograph 98, to create a smooth appearance. When using thinning shears, they must always be used close to the skin, never on the tips of the coat.

FRONT FEET AND LEGS: Comb out the hair on the front feet. Use scissors to clean out the hair between the pads on the underside of each foot. Then scissor a neat, round line around the paw as you did on each back foot. Scissor any untidy ends and shape each front leg round and cylindrical-looking, as shown in Photograph 99.

Photograph 99. The front feet should be trimmed to roundness. Work for a cylindrical look here. Be sure to scissor around, under and between the pads.

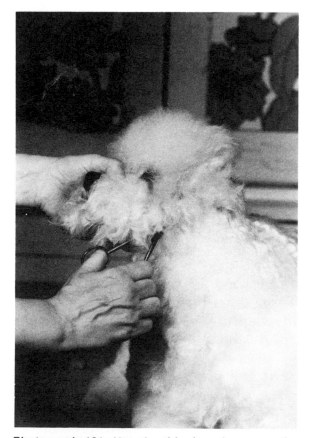

Photograph 101. Use the thinning shears on the face furnishings only if they are clumpy and do so with great care. It is a big mistake to overthin a Bichon's face furnishings.

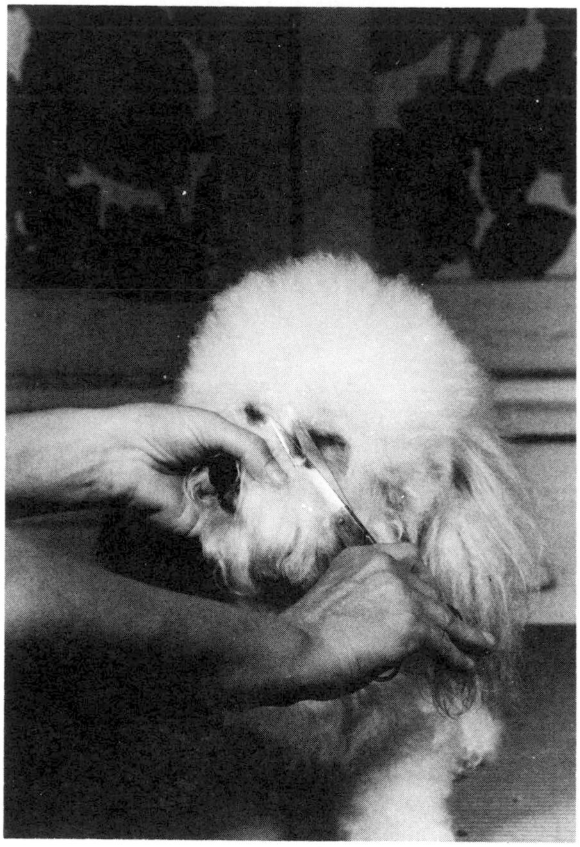

Photograph 100. Using scissors, clear the hair from the inner corner of the eyes. Proper trimming here does a great deal to enhance the Bichon Frise's captivating expression.

Photograph 102. The topknot should be round and follow the contour of the dog's skull. Trim in front of the eyes as shown to remove stray wisps and enhance expression. Obviously, great care and firm control are necessary to avoid injury at this time, particularly with puppies or dogs not accustomed to being groomed.

Photograph 103. The finished Bichon head. This dog's head has been trimmed in strictest conformity with the standard. It is properly round and reflects the complete charm of this delightful breed. Note that more hair is left on the muzzle and underjaw than on the topknot.

THE HEAD AND EARS: The Bichon Frise's head should look round. It is never trimmed to appear long and refined or square-shaped. All the head work is done with scissors and thinning shears. Comb out the hair on the face. As shown in Photograph 100, clear the hair from the inner corners of the eyes with scissors. Do not scissor under the eyes, only trim across the bridge of the nose and at the inner corners of the eyes to remove any hairs that might obscure the eyes. Next, comb out the hair on the sides of the face and in front of the ears. If this hair is thick and makes the Bichon appear "cheeky," use thinning shears, as shown in Photograph 101, to make the ears lie close to the head. Do not overthin in this area!

The shape of the topknot follows the natural, round shape of the skull. It must not be scissored flat on top. Begin by combing the hair upward and forward. As shown in Photograph 102, shorten the topknot slightly in front with scissors, to prevent hair from falling into the eyes. Next, shape the rest of the head. The hair should increase in length toward the center and back of the skull, with more hair remaining in the center of the head and tapering to the sides. The hair at the back of the skull blends with the hair on the neck. The topknot at the sides of the head, blends into the hair on the ears. There is never a scissored separation between the topknot and the ears.

Photograph 104. The finished Bichon Frise. This trimming should present a round, almost ethereal, look. Regular coat care and a little practice will quickly bring the necessary skill toward achieving the perfection shown in this photo.

Ear feathering is left long and full. Photograph 103 shows the front view of the finished head.

MOUSTACHE AND BEARD: The moustache and beard should be combed out and downward. If necessary, tip off any straggly edges, but no more than that. Photograph 104 shows the finished Bichon Frise.

SUGGESTIONS FOR COAT CARE:

Many Bichons get discolored hair near the eyes and mouth. Daily care will help control this stain. Refer to the chapter on Hair Stains.

The Bichon's coat is long and almost non-shedding. However, the coat is a double one which means the presence of an undercoat. This is a breed, therefore, that needs regular attention from puppyhood on. A puppy from four to 10 months old needs to be brushed about three times per week. Before each brushing, the coat should be sprayed with a protein conditioner or coat dressing. About every two weeks, the puppy should be bathed and brushed dry with the electric dryer. Once a month, the outer coat (or guard hairs) should be scissored. These guard hairs on the Bichon puppy grow faster than the rest of the hair and must be tipped back to make the coat grow out evenly.

Some time between the ages of 10 and 14 months, the hair may seem to mat regularly. The undercoat seems thicker, while the top hair may appear sparse. This means that the coat is changing from puppy texture to adult texture. The change is a gradual one, taking a few months and during this period, you may need to brush the hair more often to keep it from tangling. Once the coat change is complete, maintenance of the adult coat should consist of thorough brushings two to three times per week and regular shampoos before shows.

On the day of the show, spray the coat with Ring 5 Whitener/Cleaner. Allow the powder to remain in the coat for about fifteen to twenty minutes, then brush out. Be sure all traces of powder are removed from the coat before the dog enters the ring.

The Brussels Griffon

Description of Coat

The Breed Standard describes the smooth and rough Griffon coats in this way: "There are 2 distinct types of coat—rough and smooth. The rough coat should be wiry and dense, the harder and more wiry the better. On no account should the dog look or feel woolly and there should be no silky hair anywhere. The coat should not be so long as to give a shaggy appearance, but should still be distinctly different all over from the smooth coat. The head should be covered with wiry hair slightly longer around the eyes, nose, cheeks and chin, thus forming a fringe. The smooth coat is similar to that of the Boston Terrier and Bulldog, with no traces of wire hair."

Grooming the Smooth Brussels Griffon

The smooth Brussels Griffon requires a minimum of grooming. The easiest way to keep the coat in good condition is to brush regularly with the rubber brush or medium soft bristle brush described in the Equipment Chapter for short-haired breeds. Follow directions in the Brushing Chapter for short-haired breeds.

If brushed regularly, the smooth Griffon seldom needs a bath. An occasional rubdown with a terry towel moistened with Coat Dressing will keep the coat clean. When shampooing is necessary, follow instructions in the Bathing Chapter, using a tearless shampoo to help prevent eye irritation. After bathing and drying, any shaggy or unruly hairs on the body or end of the tail may be trimmed with thinning shears. The edges of the cropped ears may be scissored to make them appear neat.

The smooth Griffon's eyes are large and set in shallow sockets. This type of eye can be irritated easily and requires daily care. Refer to the Chapter on Eye Care for suggestions. Once a month, trim the nails, clean the ears and check the anal glands. Photograph 105 shows the finished smooth Brussels Griffon.

Grooming the Rough Brussels Griffon

The rough Brussels Griffon has a harsh, double coat. On this type of coat, the dead hair must be removed periodically to allow new hair to grow in. To preserve the rough Griffon's coat texture and color, the grooming process is best accomplished by hand stripping or plucking, regardless of whether the dog is a pet or show dog. Many groomers use clippers on rough Griffons as an economical and time-saving grooming

Photograph 105. The smooth variety of the Brussels Griffon, also known as the *Bra-bancon*, requires the same simple grooming as any of the other smooth coated Toy breeds.

Photograph 106. The rough Brussels Griffon is the more familiar of the two varieties of the breed. It carries a soft, furry coat next to the skin and a harsy, wiry outer jacket. Plucking or stripping, as done on the double-coated terriers, is the preferred trimming method.

method. But, if you plan to show your Brussels Griffon, never clip the head or body as clipping cuts off the ends of the hair without removing the dead undercoat, resulting in a soft coat texture and faded coat color. The only part that may be clipped on the show dog is the stomach.

Necessary Grooming Tools

The rough Griffon's coat should be stripped with a stripping comb or plucked with fingers and thumb. If you use the stripping method, you need two stripping combs; one with medium teeth for working on the body and legs, and the second with fine teeth for the head area. Do not use any type of stripper with a blade inside as this tends to cut off the hair and create a two-toned look to the coat.

You also need a natural bristle brush and the terrier palm as described in the Equipment Chapter, one pair of scissors and the half-fine, half-medium combination comb described in the Equipment Chapter.

How to Strip the Coat

Stripping the coat is done in various stages over a period of about eight to 10 weeks on the show dog, depending on the desired coat length. On the pet, the stripping process may be done in one grooming session. The hair should be stripped when it has "blown," or more simply, when the old, dead hair stands out from the body in the process of shedding. At this stage, the dead hair can be removed easily with no discomfort to the dog. To save time, before stripping, place the teeth of the stripping comb into the coat and use it all over the dog's body in the direction of the hair growth as a regular comb to remove as much of the loose, dead undercoat as possible. Combing in this manner is termed "carding" and makes the stripping process a lot faster and easier.

Stripping is easier also if you chalk the hair before you begin. Chalk tends to dry the natural oil on the coat and add a harsher texture, giving you a better grip on the hair as you strip. You may use either of two methods before stripping:
1. Ring 5 Whitener-Cleaner. An aerosol product which is sprayed lightly onto the hair.
2. Block Chalk. Apply by rubbing the block in long sweeping motions over the coat.

The correct position for holding the stripping knife is shown in the Equipment Chapter. Begin by ruffling up a bit of the coat between the blade and your thumb, as shown in Photograph 107. Press your thumb firmly against the hair and the blade, pulling the hair straight back in the direction that it grows to strip out the dead coat. Do not use the knife in an upward motion, as this cuts off the coat instead of pulling out the dead hair. Always strip in the direction that the coat grows. Work on small sections at a time until the entire stripping is completed.

Plucking Technique

Plucking means removing the dead hair with your thumb and index finger. This is done by grasping a few hairs firmly between your index finger and thumb, holding the hair near the skin, as shown in Photograph 108, and pulling backward with a slight twisting motion. Plucking is often used for the sensitive areas on the head and ears.

After stripping or plucking, make certain that all Whitener-Cleaner or chalk is brushed out of the coat.

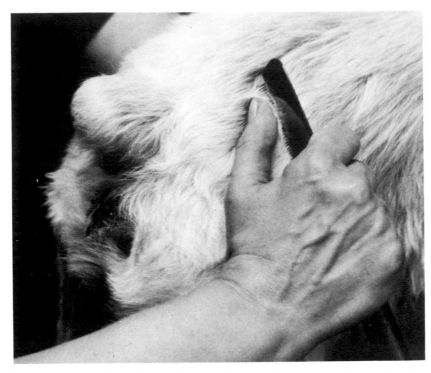

Photograph 107. Stripping is the term given to the process of removing the coat with a knife. The knife must be dull so as not to cut the hair. Cut, the coat will be of uneven color and look generally moth-eaten.

Photograph 108. Plucking the removal of coat using finger and thumb. It has been termed a *dying art* and there are few who can really do it well. It takes, time, patience and a knowledge of coats and how they grow. The rewards of plucking are the quality of the prime coat in a hand-plucked dog and the incomparable finish it imparts.

Stripping the Body and Neck

It seems more comfortable and acceptable to the dog to begin stripping behind the ears and work backwards to the tail, leaving the head to be done last. As shown in the following stripping chart, shorten the hair on the back and sides of the neck. Strip the shoulders short to make the dog appear sleek. Strip from the shoulders downward to the elbows. At the place where the front legs join the body, be careful to remove all straggly hairs to keep the dog from looking "out" at the elbows. The hair on the front of the chest and throat is stripped short. The body hair should be stripped close and the hair on the brisket should be slightly longer. As the stripping progresses, taper the short body hair so that it blends into the longer hair under the brisket. Do not leave too much hair in the brisket area as this tends to make the dog appear long and low, when the opposite effect is desired. However, do not take off too much hair and make the dog look "shelly" and without substance.

Stripping is not difficult if you know the type of coat you are working on. Some Griffon coats grow long before they "blow" and are ready to be stripped, while others "blow" and are ready for stripping before they grow long. After a few months of working on your Griffon, you should know when your dog's coat is right for stripping and then it often will be necessary only to remove the dead hair without long, tedious stripping sessions.

Stripping the Tail

Strip the hair on all sides of the tail stump.

Stripping the Hindquarters, Back Legs and Front Legs

The hair on the hindquarters and under the tail should be stripped to give a compact, short-bodied appearance. The long, dead coat on the back legs should be stripped down to the hock joint. The hair on the inside of the thighs is stripped close to create the appearance of width. When viewed from the rear, hindquarters should appear like an inverted "U". When viewed from the side, the hindquarters should appear powerful, and the legs strong with well-muscled thighs and good angulation. The forelegs should be stripped of excess hair. When trimming the forelegs, they should appear straight when viewed from any angle.

Trimming the Feet

Scissor the hair from between the pads underneath each foot. Then place the foot down in a normal standing position and scissor around the foot to make it appear round and compact looking.

Trimming the Stomach

Clip the stomach with a #10 or #15 blade. Be sure to clip only the stomach hair and not the brisket coat.

Trimming the Ears

The ears should appear sleek. All long hairs should be plucked short by hand or stripped with the fine-tooth comb. Any long hairs at the front and base of each ear should be stripped. Scissor around the edge of each ear to remove straggly hairs and make the ears appear neat.

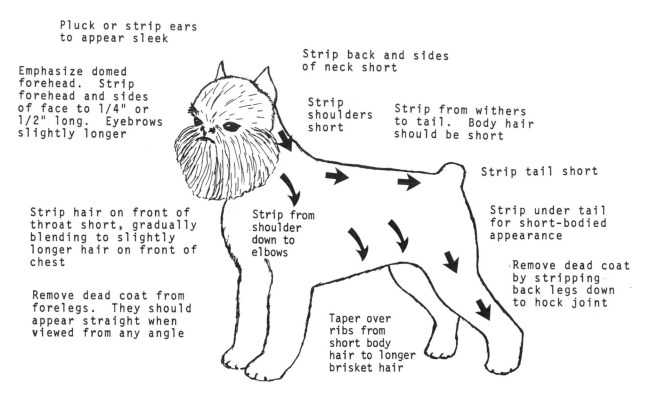

Pluck or strip ears
to appear sleek

Strip back and sides
of neck short

Emphasize domed
forehead. Strip
forehead and sides
of face to 1/4" or
1/2" long. Eyebrows
slightly longer

Strip
shoulders
short

Strip from withers
to tail. Body hair
should be short

Strip tail short

Strip hair on front of
throat short, gradually
blending to slightly
longer hair on front of
chest

Strip from
shoulder
down to
elbows

Strip under tail
for short-bodied
appearance

Remove dead coat
by stripping
back legs down
to hock joint

Remove dead coat from
forelegs. They should
appear straight when
viewed from any angle

Taper over
ribs from
short body
hair to longer
brisket hair

Diagram 12. Brussels Griffon Trimming Chart

Care of the Eyes

The rough Griffon's eyes are large, set in shallow sockets and require daily care. Refer to the Eye Care Chapter for instructions. This type of large eye can be irritated easily by wisps of long hair touching the eyeball. To prevent this from happening, shorten the hair at the inside corners of the eyes near the stop by plucking with your thumb and index finger. Do not overpluck. Shorten the hair just enough to keep the long ends from falling into the eyes. When plucked properly, the hair at the stop should resemble a small fan between the eyes. *Never cut this hair with scissors.*

Trimming the Head

Correct trimming is necessary to achieve the rough Griffon's unique expression. The long hair on the skull is stripped with the fine-tooth comb to emphasize the domed forehead. The hair on the forehead and sides of the face should be about 1/4" to 1/2" long, with eyebrows slightly longer. The beard should be profuse. To explain the easiest way to determine the beard line, locate the tiny facial mole slightly behind the corner of the mouth on each side of the face. Set the beard line from the outside corner of each eye to encircle the mouth on a line with these cheek moles. The beard should always be combed forward. When finished, the eyebrows, cheek hair and beard blend together to create the fringe around the face described in the Breed Standard. Photograph 109 illustrates correct facial grooming.

Photograph 106 shows the finished rough Brussels Griffon.

Photograph 109. The head is the Brussels Griffon's most distinctive feature. Careful study should be made of photos and well-trimmed dogs along with plentiful amounts of practice to bring the best features of head and expression out in one's own dog.

Clipping the Pet Griffon

If you do not wish to strip the pet's hair, the body coat may be clipped with a #7 or #8-1/2 blade. The head may be clipped with the #10 blade. After clipping, the undercoat is carded with the stripping comb by placing the teeth into the coat and combing in the direction of hair growth to remove all dead hair. Legs can be scissored to shape.

Bathing the Rough Griffon

If the coat is brushed properly about three times per week, the rough Brussels Griffon will rarely need a bath. On show dogs, bathing is done rarely, as shampooing softens the coat. If a shampoo is necessary for the show dog, always bathe at least 10 days before exhibition to allow the harsh texture to return to the hair. If the legs or underbody areas are dirty, they can be sponged easily without wetting the entire dog. For both pets and show dogs, when a bath is necessary, follow shampoo directions found in the Bathing Chapter. Use a texturizer or protein shampoo, bathe twice and rinse well. Do not use a creme rinse. Follow directions for drying found in the Bathing Chapter.

Suggestions for Miscellaneous Care and Coat Maintenance

While the puppy coat is growing and for adult maintenance, the hair should be brushed thoroughly from two to three times a week. Use the natural bristle brush on the body coat and the slicker brush on the furnishings and during excessive shedding periods. Before brushing, always moisten the hair with an aerosol protein conditioner or coat dressing.

After stripping or in warm weather, if there are skin irritations, Ring 5 Medicated Spray or a medicated shampoo will help to relieve stripping irritations, clipper rash, itching, summer-type rashes and other non-specific types of dermatitis.

In between shows, the Brussels Griffon's coat can be maintained in light oil to keep the furnishings from matting. A protein-lanolin formulation is best as this type of preparation is not greasy, repairs damaged hairs and, with regular use, adds body to the coat.

Once a month the nails should be trimmed, ears cleaned and anal glands checked.

In the summer months, do not exercise your Griffon in direct sunlight, as this will affect coat color. Always take the dog outside in the shade or in the early morning or at sundown to prevent fading.

Puppy Coats

As soon as the puppy's hair is long enough, it should be brushed about three times per week. At about four months of age, puppies usually begin shedding. At this time, you should pluck out the dead hair to encourage new growth. If the coat is soft, particularly on the forehead, it should be plucked often to help encourage better texture. If the puppy is brushed and combed regularly, the coat comes out gradually and long stripping sessions are not necessary. As the dog grows older, the best way to improve texture is to completely strip the coat twice a year. If the dog is not being shown, this is best accomplished during the normal shedding periods. To maintain the profuse facial furnishings, and keep the beard from discoloring or tangling, several times a week after the dog finishes eating, spray the beard with a liquid detangler and comb gently.

Preparing the Rough Brussels Griffon for Show

Stripping a Brussels Griffon for show is done in various stages over a period of several weeks, depending on desired coat length. Show stripping is more time consuming than pet stripping. It is difficult to recommend exactly when to begin stripping the show coat, but the following guidelines may be used until you can determine how long it takes your Griffon's coat to grow in. Coat types vary according to inherited texture, climate and humidity. About seven to ten weeks before the show, strip the hair on the ribs and tail. On the back legs, strip down to the hock joint. One to two weeks later, strip the neck, back and hindquarters. At this time, strip the ears, throat, and sides of the face behind the beard.

One week before the show, some additional work is necessary with finger and thumb. Pluck out any dead hairs on the body and legs. Pluck and shape the leg furnishings. Tidy up the ears and scissor the edges to look neat. Trim the feet. Strip out any unruly hairs on the tail. Shorten the hair on the front of the chest and hindquarters to emphasize the short body. Shorten the hair at the inside corners of the eyes and tidy the hair on the cheeks and forehead.

On the day of the show, spray the hair lightly with an aerosol protein conditioner and brush with the natural bristle brush to add sheen.

The Cavalier King Charles Spaniel

Description of Coat

The Breed Standard describes the coat as "long and silky and very soft to the touch; free from curl, though a slight wave is permissible. Feathering on ears, legs and tail should be long, and the feathering on the feet is a feature of the breed. No trimming of the dog is permitted. However, it is permissible, and often desirable, to remove the hair growing between the pads on the underside of the foot."

Brushing and Combing

Follow brushing and combing instructions for Toy Spaniels found in the Brushing Chapter. Remember to brush the body hair thoroughly against the growth of the hair (from tail to head). This is especially important to remove excessive dead hair during the early summer shedding time. Finish by brushing with the growth of hair, from the head to the tail, and down the legs.

Eye Care

Because the Cavalier's eyes are large and round, they should be cleaned and checked daily for irritation. Refer to the Eye Care Chapter.

Miscellaneous

Clean ears, cut nails and check anal glands before bathing or at least once a month.

Bathing and Drying

If a Cavalier is brushed and combed properly several times a week, it will not need to be bathed often. However, show dogs should be bathed one or two days before exhibition. Follow instructions in the Bathing Chapter, giving two shampoos and washing the head with a tearless shampoo. Since the Standard calls for a long, silky coat, use a creme rinse after the bath.

Correct drying of the Cavalier King Charles Spaniel is important. Using a blower/dryer, brush the hair in the direction of its growth as the hot air blows on the coat. The hair must be brushed completely dry. The Cavalier's coat has a tendency to curl when wet and, if a show dog is not properly dried, you may end up with a mass

Photograph 110. The Cavalier King Charles Spaniel is a natural breed requiring no trimming. His flat-lying coat should brushed regularly to bring out its shine and bloom.

of ringlets instead of a long, silky coat. If too much curl is evident after the dog is dry, wrap a terry towel around the body and hips, pin it together to flatten the hair and leave it on all night while the dog sleeps. Next morning, remove the towel and the coat will lay flat. If necessary, do this every night before the show.

Finishing

Use scissors to cut out the excess hair between the pads underneath the feet. Do not scissor any hair off the tops of the feet as they should appear profusely feathered. Whiskers may or may not be trimmed, according to your personal preference. Any unruly clumps of hair at the base of the skull or under the ears should be thinned with thinning shears. Comb the ear feathering, body and leg feathering downward. Photograph 110 shows the finished Cavalier King Charles Spaniel.

Coat Care

In between groomings, condition the coat with an aerosol protein conditioner, following instructions found in the Brushing Chapter. All white areas may be sprayed with Ring 5 Whitener-Cleaner. Allow the powder to remain in the coat for a few minutes, then brush out with a bristle brush.

The Chihuahua

The Chihuahua comes in two varieties, short-haired (called "Smooth Coat") and long-haired. Smooth coated Chihuahuas are more popular then the long coated variety. Structurally, the two varieties are the same.

Care of the Pet Dog—Smooth Coat

The Chihuahua requires a minimum of trimming. As is the case with all short-haired breeds, the most important factor comes from within. Feeding your dog properly, plus regular conditioning, is the basis for a healthy, shining coat. The easiest way to keep the coat in good condition is to brush regularly with a fine-quality bristle brush. Use medium-soft bristles that will not scratch the dog but will get into the skin to remove the dead hair and dirt. Follow directions for "Short-Haired Dogs" in the Brushing Chapter.

Once a month, pet Chihuahuas should have nails trimmed, ears cleaned, teeth and anal glands checked and whiskers trimmed. A short-haired dog seldom needs a bath if groomed regularly. An occasional rubdown with a sponge or terry towel moistened with a Dri-Bath Shampoo or Coat Dressing will keep the coat lustrous and clean. When bathing is necessary, follow instructions found in the Bathing Chapter.

Care of the Show Dog—Smooth Coat

The authors of *The Complete Chihuahua* (published by Howell Book House), in describing the smooth coat, state that "all kinds of short coats are found on Chihuahuas, although there is one characteristic and correct kind of coat. This is a very dense, fur-like coat, very short and smooth over the head and ears, with a kind of short ruff over the neck and shoulders, shortening on the body again and longer on the tail. The dog should be free from naked or nearly naked areas which are so often found on short-haired toy dogs of other breeds. The Chihuahua coat is not close fitting, but rather tends slightly to stand away from the skin. The hair colors are absolutely immaterial. Black, white, red, blue, gray, fawn, chocolate, liver, cream and tan are acceptable. Nor does the distribution of colors make any difference. There is no technical choice between solid colors and piebalds or parti-colors. Although there may be a personal choice among the colors, such personal equations are not to be presumed to affect the excellence of the dog."

A Smooth Coated Chihuahua is easy to prepare for the show ring. You should brush often with the fine-quality bristle brush mentioned before. Regular brushing removes the dead hair and stimulates the growth of new hair on a short-haired dog.

Follow these steps to prepare the Chihuahua for the show ring:

1. Check the teeth. Chihuahuas often inherit poor teeth, therefore tartar should never be allowed to accumulate or the teeth may loosen and fall out.
2. The Chihuahua is one breed that does not have the nails cut as short as possible. Long toes are characteristic of the breed. The nails should be large and strong. They are somewhat curved and, for the show ring, are left long and blunt. The nails should be cut only when they curve back toward the foot and hamper the dog's action. Then they should be cut back slightly to allow the dog to walk freely.
3. Check anal glands.
4. Bathe the dog, if necessary. Shampoo with a tearless Protein shampoo and be sure to rinse well.
5. When the dog is dry, place him on the grooming table. Use thinning shears and thin any untidy hairs on the body. With blunt-edged scissors, trim the whiskers and eyebrow hairs.

Before going into the show ring, spray the Chihuahua with Ring 5 Bright & Shine and rub down with the rubber brush described in the Equipment Chapter. This will deepen the coat color and add a gloss to the hair.

Photograph 111 shows the finished Smooth Coat Chihuahua.

Photograph 111. Coat care for the Smooth Coat Chihuahua is extremely simple, consisting of the removal of only the longest hairs that detract from overall smoothness. The breed standard mentions that nails should be moderately long. In this regard the Chihuahua differs from all other breeds.

Grooming the Long Coat Chihuahua for Show

The Breed Standard describes the long coat as "of a soft texture, either flat or slightly curly, with undercoat preferred. Ears fringed (heavily fringed ears may be tipped slightly, never down), feathering on the feet and legs, and pants on the hind legs. Large ruff on neck desired and preferred. Tail full and long (as a plume).

Photograph 112. Even the Long Coat Chihuahua is an easy grooming job. His coat requires a thorough brushing and only the removal of the feelers on the face and any uneven hairs on the feet.

Repeat all steps mentioned for Smooth Coat Chihuahuas. After the dog has been bathed, use a creme rinse. Brush dry following directions for long-coated dogs found in the Bathing Chapter. Stand the dog on the grooming table for the finishing touches. With scissors, remove any uneven hairs from the pads underneath the toes. Trim the whiskers and eyebrow hairs with blunt-edged scissors. Finish the body coat by brushing into proper position with the pin or bristle brush. Brush hair on the back towards the tail, in the direction that it grows. Brush downward and outward on the underbody fringe. Brush the feathering on the back legs outward and downward. Brush the tail plume forward over the back. Brush the feathering on the back of the front legs straight out. Brush the neck ruff upward and outward. Comb the ear fringes.

Photograph 112 shows the finished Long Coat Chihuahua.

The Chinese Crested Dog

The Chinese Crested Dog is not eligible for American Kennel Club registration at this time. Closely related to the hairless dogs of Mexico, Africa, India and Turkey, the Chinese Crested differs slightly from these breeds by having a tuft of long hair on the end of the tail and on each foot and one on the head called the "crest."

Chinese Cresteds come in a wide variety of colors over a white foundation. Sometimes, the coat looks like it is spotted with white, but you should know that white is always the basic body color. The skin of Chinese Crested puppies is very sensitive and should be bathed regularly with a rich shampoo and then oiled to keep it smooth and soft; otherwise it will become rough and cracked. Adult dogs go through a color change, depending on the time of year and exposure to the sun, similar to a human sunbathing. Adult Chinese Cresteds must be protected against exposure to the sun, since the white areas are subject to burn. If you live in a year-round hot climate, they should be rubbed with suntan oil before being allowed in the sun for any length of time.

Grooming the Chinese Crested:

1. Comb out "crest," tail hair and hair on feet.
2. Cut the toenails.
3. Clean insides of the ears with cotton swab and baby oil.
4. Check anal glands.
5. Bathe the dog, using a protein tearless shampoo.
6. When the dog is dry, rub the skin with coat oil or baby oil.
   Wipe off excess with a terry towel.
7. Dogs should be bathed and oiled regularly.

Photograph 113 shows the finished Chinese Crested Dog.

Photograph 113. The Chinese Crested Dog is one of the true oddities in the world of dogs. With his almost hairless body, grooming is more a matter of skin health than anything else. Keeping the coat oiled and away from direct sunlight are important.

The English Toy Spaniel

King Charles and Ruby, Blenheim and Prince Charles

Description of Coat

The Breed Standard describes the coat as *"long, silky, soft and wavy, but not curly. There should be a profuse mane, extending well down in the front of the chest. The feather should be well displayed on the ears and feet, and in the latter case so thickly as to give the appearance of being webbed. It is also carried well up the backs of the legs. In the Black and Tan the feather on the ears is very long and profuse, exceeding that of the Blenheim by an inch or more. The feather on the tail (which is cut to the length of about 1-1/2 inches) should be silky, and from 3 to 4 inches in length, constituting a marked 'flag' of a square shape, and not carried above the level of the back."*

Brushing and Combing

Follow brushing and combing instructions for "Toy Spaniels" found in the Brushing Chapter.

Eye Care

Since the English Toy Spaniel's eyes are large and round, they must be cleaned and checked daily for irritation. Refer to the Eye Care Chapter.

Before Bathing or Once a Month

Clean ears, cut nails and check anal glands.

Bathing and Drying

If the English Toy Spaniel is brushed and combed properly several times a week, it will not need to be bathed often. However, show dogs should be bathed one or two days before exhibition. Follow instructions in the Bathing Chapter, giving two shampoos and washing the head with a tearless shampoo. Since the Standard calls for a long, silky and soft coat, use a creme rinse after the bath.

Correct drying of the English Toy Spaniel's coat is important. Using a blower/dryer, brush the hair in the direction of its growth as the hot air blows the

Photograph 114. The English Toy Spaniel carries a coat very like that of the Cavalier King Charles Spaniel to which he is closely related. Brush work is the important feature here and will bring the coat to its finest bloom if done regularly. *Tauskey.*

coat. The hair must be brushed completely dry. This type of coat has a tendency to curl when wet and, if a show dog is not properly dried, you may end up with a mass of ringlets instead of a long, silky coat. If too much curl is evident after the dog is dry, wrap a terry towel around the body and hips, pin it together to flatten the hair and leave it on all night while the dog sleeps. Next morning, remove the towel and the coat will lay flat. If necessary do this every night before the show.

Finishing

Use scissors to cut out the excess hair between the pads underneath the feet. Do not scissor any hair off the tops of the feet as they should appear profusely feathered. Trim off facial whiskers. Any unruly clumps of hair at the base of the skull or under the ears should be thinned with thinning shears. Comb ear feathering downward. The long feathering on the front of the chest, underbody, legs and tail should be brushed downward.

Photograph 114 shows the finished English Toy Spaniel.

Coat Care

Several times a week, use an aerosol protein conditioner on the hair. Follow instructions in the Brushing Chapter. White parts can be sprayed with Ring 5 Whitener-Cleaner, then brushed out.

On show dogs, about one hour before the dog goes into the ring, spray and brush the hair with a Coat Dressing. All white and light colored parts should be sprayed with Ring 5 Whitener-Cleaner. Allow the powder to remain in the hair for a few minutes, then brush out, making sure that all traces of powder are removed from the hair.

The Italian Greyhound

Description of Coat

The Breed Standard describes the coat as follows: "Skin fine and supple, hair short, glossy like satin and soft to the touch."

Care of the Pet Dog

The Italian Greyhound requires a minimum of difficult grooming. As is the case with all short-haired breeds, the most important factor comes from within. Feeding your dog properly, supplementing his diet with vitamins and/or an internal skin and coat food supplement and regular conditioning are the basis for a healthy, shining coat. The easiest way to keep the coat in good condition is to brush regularly with a fine-quality bristle brush. Use a medium-soft brush that will not scratch the dog's skin but will remove the dead hair and dirt. Follow instructions for "Short Haired Breeds" found in the Brushing Chapter.

Once a month, the nails should be cut, ears cleaned, teeth and anal glands checked and attended to and whiskers trimmed. The Italian Greyhound seldom needs a bath if groomed regularly. An occasional rubdown with a sponge or terry towel moistened with a coat dressing or Dri-Bath Shampoo will keep the coast lustrous and clean. When bathing is necessary, follow instructions found in the Bathing Chapter.

Care of the Show Dog

If you intend to show your Italian Greyhound, there are a few additional steps to follow to prepare the dog for the ring. This additional grooming will take only a short time a day or two before the show. Follow this step-by-step procedure:

1. Bathe the dog, if necessary. Shampoo with a tearless protein shampoo and be sure to rinse well.
2. When the dog is dry, place him on the grooming table. If necessary, use clippers with a #10 blade to remove any excess hair from the stomach area. Stand the dog up on his hind legs, point clippers upward and clip from above the genitals to the middle of the dog.
3. Stand the dog on the table with the hindquarters facing you for the finishing touches, which will be done with thinning shears and blunt-edged scissors. The Italian Greyhound should have a sleek, sculptured look and, now you must go

Photograph 115. The Italian Greyhound is one of the most elegant of all breeds. He needs only regular brushing, slight trimming of the longest hairs and normal management to look his exquisite best. *Ludwig.*

over the dog from head to tail, trimming off any untidy hairs that stick out to spoil this outline. *The Italian Greyhound's coat is thin and glossy like satin, so there will not be much trimming necessary to attain a sleek look. Do be careful not to over-trim and make bare spots!* Start by removing any uneven hairs from the back feet and pads underneath the toes. Check the back of the hind legs, hindquarters, tail, body (especially the tuck-up and brisket) and thin any uneven hairs that stick out to spoil the sleek look.

4. Turn the dog around to stand facing you. Remove any uneven hairs from the front feet and pads underneath the toes. Check elbows, front of chest and shoulders and thin any untidy hairs that spoil the sculptured outline.

5. Do the head area last. With blunt-edged scissors, remove the whiskers. Thin any shaggy tufts of hair at the base of the ears, if necessary.

On the day of the show, before going into the ring, spray the coat with Ring 5 Bright & Shine and rub with the rubber brush described in the Equipment Chapter. This will add a gloss to the coat.

Photograph 115 shows the finished Italian Greyhound.

The Japanese Spaniel

Description of Coat

The Breed Standard describes the coat as "profuse, long, straight, rather silky. It should be absolutely free from wave or curl and not lie too flat, but have a tendency to stand out, especially at the neck so as to give a thick mane or ruff, which with profuse feathering on the thighs and tail, gives a very showy appearance."

Brushing and Combing

The correct brush for the Japanese Spaniel is a small size pin or natural bristle brush. Follow directions for "Toy Spaniels" found in the Brushing Chapter.

The correct comb is the half-fine and half-medium tooth comb described in the Equipment Chapter. When the hair had been thoroughly brushed, comb through the coat to be sure all mats and tangles are removed.

Eye Care

The Japanese Spaniel has large, rather prominent eyes which should be cleaned daily and checked for any signs of irritation. Refer to the Eye Care Chapter.

Before Bathing or Once Every Month

Clean ears, cut nails and check anal glands.

Bathing and Drying

A pet Japanese Spaniel that is brushed and combed properly will not need to be bathed often. However, a show dog must be bathed one or two days before the show. Follow instructions in the Bathing Chapter, using a whitener shampoo on the body and a tearless shampoo on the head. Rinse well and follow with a creme rinse.

Use a blower/dryer to dry the hair. While the heat blows on the coat, brush the hair with a pin or bristle brush. When the hair is partially dry, brush it against the growth (from the tail to the head). As you do this, the hair will naturally fall back into place, but the coat will stand out more. Be sure to dry the facial wrinkle completely. If there is any staining on the white facial hair, use white Eyetek immediately after the dog is dry to prevent further discoloration.

Photograph 116. The Japanese Spaniel is a typical representative of the short-faced breeds of the Far East. Unlike the Toy Spaniels of Europe, the Japanese Spaniel should have a slightly off-standing coat. Therefore, in grooming always work with this feature in mind to make a dog as showy as possible.

Finishing

Use scissors to cut out the excess hair between the pads under the feet. With each foot in a normal standing position on the grooming table, scissor the sides of the foot only, not the hair near the toenails. The Standard describes the feet as small and shaped somewhat long with feathering tufts that should not increase the width of the foot, but only the length. Brush the leg feathering outward and downward. On pets only, you may scissor off any straggly tips on the leg feathering. Fluff up the tail plume, allowing it to fall over the back. The hair on the head and back should be brushed flat, but the mane is brushed in an upward and outward motion to give the appearance of fullness. Ear feathering should be brushed downward. Scissor off facial whiskers and those over the eyes.

Photograph 116 shows the finished Japanese Spaniel

Suggestions for Coat Care

A protein aerosol conditioner is best for maintaining the coat. This preparation should be sprayed on the hair several times a week as the coat is brushed.

For show dogs, about an hour before the dog goes into the ring, spray all white parts of the coat with Ring 5 Whitener-Cleaner. Brush the hair as instructed above, making sure all traces of the powder are out of the coat before the dog goes into the ring.

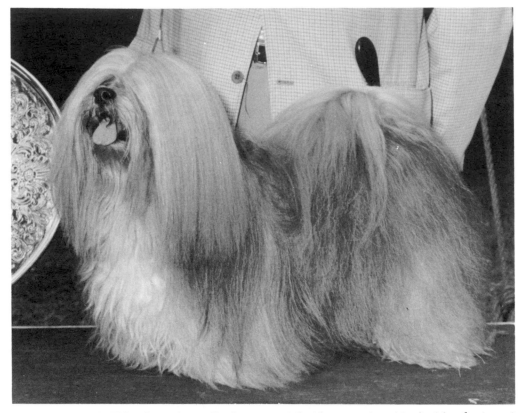

Photograph 117. This Lhasa Apso displays a coat that is correct and typical for the breed. To achieve such bloom, many hours of regular grooming must be devoted to the dog. It is possible, however, to have a well-groomed pet without using the very meticulous procedures for show dogs. *Gilbert.*

Photograph 118. This poor creature is a Lhasa Apso whose coat has been completely neglected over an extended period. Simple, regularly-scheduled brushing would have kept him clean and well-groomed. It will take considerable work to put his coat right now.

The Lhasa Apso

Description of Coat

The breed standard describes the Lhasa Apso's coat as "Heavy, straight, hard, not woolly nor silky, of good length and very dense." There should be heavy head furnishings with good fall over the eyes, good whiskers and beard. The ears should be pendant and heavily feathered. Both forelegs and hind legs should be heavily furnished with hair. Feet are well-feathered and should be round and cat-like with good pads. The tail is well-feathered and carried well over the back.

Grooming Instructions

The Lhasa Apso shown in Photograph 117 is in show coat. Photograph 118 shows a side view of a neglected pet Lhasa Apso. Basically, the grooming procedure is the same and both dogs will be used to illustrate this chapter where necessary. Special pointers for caring for the show coat are found at the end of the grooming instructions.

Brushing and Combing

The correct brush for the Lhasa Apso is a natural bristle or pin brush. On matted pets like the dog shown in this chapter, you may need to use a medium size slicker brush to remove tangles. Since any type of wire brush can break off the ends of the long hair, do brush with a light stroke when working on a matted pet. The correct comb is the half-fine and half-medium style illustrated in the Equipment Chapter. You will also need an extra-fine tooth comb for the beard area.

A study of the head area of the pet indicates that there is an accumulation of food and dirt caked in the beard and that the fall is badly matted. To prevent loss of hair when grooming such a tangled dog, rub tangle remover or baby oil into the matted areas to loosen the dirt, while you brush the body and legs first.

The Lhasa Apso's coat must be brushed thoroughly so that all mats and tangles are removed before bathing. The long body coat is brushed in the layering method described and illustrated in the Brushing Chapter.

Sit the dog on the grooming table to brush the head area. Brush the fall away from

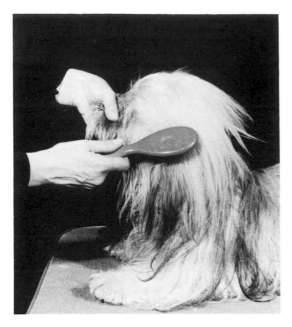

Photograph 119. Begin grooming by brushing back the fall from the eyes. A pin brush will remove most of the mats that have formed if a spray de-tangler has been used on the coat first.

the eyes, as shown in Photograph 119. Brush ear feathering downward. Brush the hair on the sides of the head and muzzle, taking care not to injure the eyes with the bristles or pins on the brush.

After the hair has been thoroughly brushed, go through the coat with the medium-tooth part of the comb to be sure all mats have been removed. Photograph 120 shows the use of the extra-fine tooth comb removing matter near the eye corners on the matted pet. If you soaked this area with oil before brushing, the dirt and foreign matter should be easy to remove.

Pre-Bath Preparations

Clean ears and check eyes for irritation. Cut toenails and check anal glands.

Bathing and Drying

Before putting the dog into the water, use the edge of the comb to part the hair down the center of the back from head to tail, letting the long coat fall to each side.

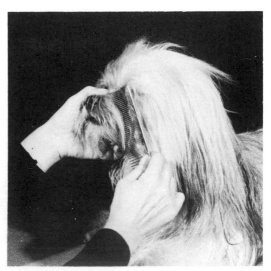

Photograph 120. Use the fine teeth of a half and half comb to remove accumulated matter from eye corners.

Follow instructions found in the Bathing Chapter. Give two shampoos. Use a tearless shampoo on the head area. When washing the body, always keep the part in the center of the back to prevent tangling. If the beard and hair under the eyes are badly stained, dip a toothbrush into the shampoo and gently scrub these areas. Rinse all traces of soap out of the coat. A creme rinse is optional. If you do use a rinse, select a brand that has been formulated to make the coat hang straight. Always brush the coat dry. While the dryer blows on the wet hair, keep the part in the center of the back as you brush each side downward in the direction that the hair grows.

Finishing the Lhasa Apso

STOMACH: This step in Lhasa grooming is optional and a matter of personal preference. To keep the genital area clean and prevent hair staining, clip the stomach with a #10 or #15 blade. Start just above the genitals and clip off a little hair. Do not clip too high up and cut off any long feathering under the chest.

FEET: Scissor the hair from between the pads underneath each foot, as shown in Photograph 121. Then place the foot down in a normal standing position. Holding up any long leg hair with your free hand, comb the hair on the foot, fanning the coat out in a large circle. Scissor off any straggly hairs which detract from the round shape. Never over-scissor the feet as they should be well-feathered.

BODY: Use the comb edge or knitting needle as shown in Photograph 122, to part the hair down the center of the back from the top of the head to the base of the tail. Brush or comb the long hair on each side of the part straight down. When the part is straight, spray the back with a light mist of coat dressing, aerosol protein conditioner or the "dry type" hair spray made for men. Comb the hair on the front of the chest downward. On the pet Lhasa Apso only, if there are untidy hairs under the tail, these must never be scissored or clipped off, but may be thinned with thinning shears, as shown in Photograph 123 to make this area appear neat.

TAIL: Brush the tail forward, letting the long feathering fall over the back.

HEAD: Begin at the top of the head and continue the part line straight down to the top of the nose. Photograph 124 shows the head parted and combed. If the Lhasa Apso is a pet, you may pull the fall up and fasten it with a rubber band or barrette. Photographs and directions for pulling up the hair above the eyes can be found in the Yorkshire Terrier or Shih Tzu chapters. Photograph 125 shows the finished Lhasa Apso.

Suggestions for Coat Care

The Lhasa Apso should be brushed regularly at least three times a week. Regular brushing removes the dead hair before it has a chance to mat at the skin. Climate seems to influence how much dead hair a Lhasa Apso accumulates. If the dog is not brushed regularly, the dead hair will mat and cause serious coat problems.

Growing and maintaining a show coat can be difficult for a novice. The puppy should be brushed from two to three times a week. Always use a coat conditioner or coat dressing before you brush the hair to reduce static electricity and coat breakage. While your puppy is young, get him accustomed to having the hard-to-get spots brushed and combed under the chest, under the front and back legs and on the beard.

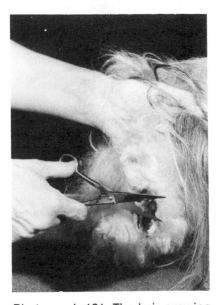

Photograph 121. The hair growing between the foot pads should be cleaned out with scissors. Excess amounts of hair between the pads of heavy-coated dogs will cause the foot to spread and catch seeds, pebbles, chewing gum and similar material which can cause discomfort and even lameness.

Photograph 122. Use the end of a comb or a knitting needle to make a part down the center of the Lhasa's back. After the part is straight, spray the hair to keep it in place.

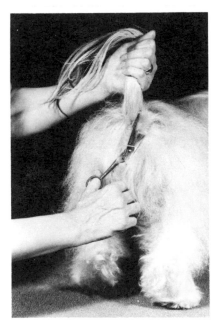

Photograph 123. If your Lhasa is a pet it is permissible to use thinning shears around the vent for hygenic purposes.

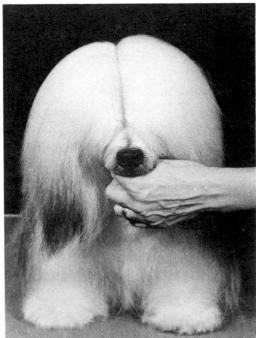

Photograph 124. Here is the finished head. Some owners prefer to catch up the head fall in a barette or elastic. Show dogs head furnishings are also wrapped or otherwise kept out of the dog's eyes at home.

Photograph 125. This is the finished Lhasa Apso pet. Certainly he does not carry the glorious coat of the show champion illustrated earlier in the chapter. But his coat is in order, he is comfortable and he looks like a Lhasa Apso.

The puppy should be bathed every 10 days to two weeks. Eyes need attention every day. If you own a male Lhasa and have a problem with stained or matted feathering under the body from urine residue, sponge off the stomach every other day in between the regular shampoos. In place of spongings, you may also use Ring 5 Whitener-Cleaner on the long underbody feathering.

As the Lhasa's coat starts getting longer, keep the hair oiled in between shows to encourage growth and prevent breakage. Use a light oil in aerosol form, such as Ring 5, Pro-Groom, St. Aubrey Coatasheen or Mr. Groom. If you wish to use a slightly heavier oil, try St. Aubrey Royal Coatalin, Alpha Keri or Lubath (these last two are purchased in a drug store). The Royal Coatalin comes in paraffin block form and is applied by first running the pin brush through the block, then through the hair. Royal Coatalin may also be melted on the top of the stove in a pie pan and brushed into the hair in liquid form. The Lubath is poured directly from the bottle onto the coat and brushed into the hair. The Alpha Keri is best applied after the dog has been bathed and rinsed. While the Lhasa Apso is still wet, immediately before you remove him from the tub, pour the following mixture over the coat. Mix one capful of Alpha Keri with four cups warm water (you may add creme rinse to this mixture) and stir the mixture enough to make the oil and water blend. Squeeze the Alpha Keri mixture through the hair to be sure all areas are saturated. Take the dog out of the tub and dry as usual. Remember, however, that when you show your Lhasa Apso, it must be bathed before the show and no oil of any type rinsed into the coat.

Never over-oil the hair. This only clogs the pores and slows down hair growth. When keeping a show dog in any oil preparation, it is best to bathe every two weeks to prevent excessive dirt build-up caused by oil on the hair.

During the change from puppy to adult coat, the hair seems to mat overnight and must be brushed daily to prevent coat loss. To help brushing during the coat change, spray the hair with a coat dressing or light oil, set your dryer on "Cool" and allow it to blow on the coat as you brush in layers.

If you allow your Lhasa Apso to become badly matted, it is best to cut the hair down to a length of about two inches and keep that hair oiled and brushed. In a few months, you will notice how fast the hair grows back.

As soon as the fall is long enough, it should be wrapped to encourage growth and prevent breakage. In between shows, the long body coat and ear feathering may also be wrapped to protect the ends of the hair and prevent damage. Instructions and photographs are found in the Chapter entitled "Wrapping The Show Coat."

If you are troubled with stained hair, refer to the Chapter "How To Treat Stained Hair" for suggestions for Lhasa Apsos.

Before the Show

The Lhasa Apso usually requires a bath before exhibition. The best time to bathe the dog is the evening before the show. Once the coat is dry, it is important that you keep the hair on the legs and feet from becoming dirty or stained. Always confine the dog (cage or exercise pen) in an area covered with white paper or white towels. Never use newspaper! The ink used for printing newspapers is usually the cheapest kind, mainly oil with lampblack. Putting a clean light-colored dog on newspaper will usually result in inkstains on the underbody, legs and feet. Most exhibitors prefer using the type of white paper used in physicians' offices to cover examination tables. This kind of paper comes on rolls and can be found at any medical supply house.

The day of the show, the coat should be brushed with a coat dressing which does not contain oil or alcohol. All white or light-colored areas may be sprayed with Ring 5 Whitener-Cleaner and brushed thoroughly to remove all traces of powder from the coat. Any stained areas around the eyes can be touched up with EyeTek before the dog goes into the ring.

The Maltese

Description of Coat

The Breed Standard describes the coat as "single, that is, without undercoat. It hangs long, flat and silky over the sides of the body almost, if not quite, to the ground. The long head-hair may be tied up in a topknot or it may be left hanging. Any suggestion of kinkiness, curliness, or woolly texture is objectionable. Color, pure white. Light tan or lemon on the ears is permissible, but not desirable."

Brushing and Combing

The correct brush is a pin or natural bristle brush. On matted pets, you may need to use a small size slicker brush. The correct comb is the half-fine, half-medium style described in the Equipment Chapter. You will also need an extra-fine tooth comb with handle for the beard area.

Before brushing, if the beard hair is caked with food, discolored or matted, rub a little liquid tangle remover into the coat. While you brush the rest of the dog, the de-tangler will loosen mats and foreign matter, making the beard easier to brush out.

Begin by brushing the hair under the chest. Photographs and instructions for brushing the coat in the layering method are found in the "Long, Flowing Coated Breeds" section of the Brushing Chapter.

Brushing the Head

After the body hair has been brushed, sit the dog on the grooming table to brush the head. Brush the hair on the top of the head away from the eyes. Brush the hair on the sides of the head and around the mouth, taking care not to injure the eyes with the bristles or pins on the brush. Brush the ear feathering downward. Photographs are shown in the Brushing Chapter.

Combing

Once the hair has been thoroughly brushed, comb through the coat with the medium-tooth side to be sure all mats have been removed. On matted pets, if you soaked the beard hair in a liquid tangle remover before starting to brush, this area should comb out easily with no hair loss.

Eye Care

The eyes should be checked daily and cleaned of any foreign matter. Refer to the Eye Care Chapter.

Pre-Bath Preparations

Clean ears, cut toenails and check anal glands.

Bathing and Drying

Before putting the dog into the water, use the edge of the comb or a knitting needle to part the hair down the center of the back from the top of the head to the tail, letting the long coat fall to each side. Follow directions found in the Bathing Chapter for long, flowing coated breeds. Give two shampoos. Always use a whitener shampoo to keep your Maltese looking snow white, especially in the winter or under certain climatic conditions which cause some coat textures to yellow. Wash the eye area with a tearless shampoo. When washing the body, always keep the part in the center of the back to prevent tangling. If the beard and hair under the eyes are badly stained, dip a toothbrush into the shampoo and gently scrub these areas. Rinse all traces of soap out ot the coat. Do use a creme rinse to make the hair more manageable after bathing. Always brush the coat dry, following directions in the Bathing Chapter. While the dryer blows on the wet hair, keep the part in the center of the back as you brush each side downward in the direction that the hair grows.

Finishing the Maltese

STOMACH: This step is optional and a matter of personal preference. To keep the genital area clean and prevent hair staining, clip the area with a #10 or #15 blade. Clip off only a little hair. Be careful not to cut off any long feathering under the chest.

FEET: Scissor the hair from between the pads underneath each foot. Then place the foot down in a normal standing position. Holding up any long leg hair with your free hand, comb the hair on the foot, fanning the coat out in a large circle. Scissor around the foot, removing any straggly hairs which detract from the round shape. Photographs showing feet trimming are found in the Yorkshire Terrier and Shih Tzu grooming chapters.

BODY: Use the edge of the comb or a knitting needle to part the hair down the center of the back from the top of the head to the base of the tail. Brush the long hair on each side of the part straight down. When the part is straight, spray the back with a light mist of coat dressing, aerosol protein conditioner or the "dry type" hair spray made for men. Photographs showing how to part the hair down the back are found in the Shih Tzu, Lhasa Apso or Yorkshire Terrier chapters. Comb the hair on the front of the chest downward. On the pet Maltese only, if there are untidy hairs near the tail, these must never be scissored or clipped off, but may be thinned with thinning shears to make the area look neat.

TAIL: Brush the tail forward, letting the long feathering fall over the back.

Diagram 13. Tying up the Maltese topknot. The sketches in this diagram illustrate how the topknot is done in the United States. In England the topknot is usually done with one bow in the center of the head. Regardless of how you form the topknot, always use vividly-colored ribbon to set off the pure white coat.

119

HEAD: One of the distinguishing features of the Maltese is the way in which the topknot is tied up. The following materials are necessary for the topknot:

Nylon Tulle: Cut into squares, each 2-1/2" x 2-1/2". Always use soft nylon tulle rather than nylon net which is stiff and hard to work with.

Rubber Bands: Bands should be white and small enough to turn only twice.

Ribbon: 1/4" to 3/8" wide. To enhance the whiteness of the Maltese, select vibrant color ribbon in shades of purple, royal blue, red, emerald green, deep turquoise. The best ribbon to use for the bows is made of velvet, acetate or satin. To keep the bows from raveling, buy ribbon with embossed, cut edges. To do the topknots, you need to cut 2 pieces of ribbon, each about 3" in length. (You may also use colorful heavy yarn in place of ribbon bows.)

Cotton Thread: Should be the same color as your ribbon. Cut two pieces; each about 3" in length.

MAKING THE TOPKNOTS: (Diagram 13)

1. In the United States, the Maltese usually has two topknots, one above each eye. In England, however, the Maltese has a single topknot. To make two topknots, part the hair with the edge of the comb along the dotted lines shown in Sketch A.
2. Comb through one section to be sure the hairs are collected together properly and smoothly, as shown in Sketch B.
3. Fold a tulle square around the hair, as shown in Sketch C. Keep the square close to the head to enclose as many wispy ends as possible. If any wispy ends slip out from between the tulle, use a light touch of hair styling gel to keep them in place.
4. Fold the wrapped section toward the back, letting the end fall to the outer corner of the eyes, as shown in Sketch D. Fasten with a rubber band. Check to be sure that no hairs are pulled too tightly or that no folds of skin have been pulled up into the tulle wrapping.
5. Repeat this procedure on the other topknot. Sketch E shows both topknots wrapped and fastened with rubber bands.
6. Fold the ribbon into thirds, as shown in Sketch F. To hold the bows together, tie in the center with a 3" piece of cotton thread. Tie the bows onto the front of the topknot. Cut off the excess thread after the bows are attached. Photograph 126 shows the Maltese with topknots in place.
7. To make the English topknot, part the hair as instructed in #1, omitting the part between the eyes. Fasten forelocks with a white rubber band and add one bow.

Finishing the Head

Comb ear feathering downward. The facial furnishings are parted over the nose and combed to each side of the mouth. Photograph 126 shows finished view of the Maltese.

Suggestions for Coat Care

The Maltese should be brushed regularly at least three times a week. Regular brushing removes the dead hair before it has a chance to mat at the skin. If the dog is

Photograph 126. A Maltese in proper bloom is a thrilling sight. The long, cascading white coat is extremely showy and has stood the breed in good stead in top competition.

not brushed regularly, the dead hair will mat and cause serious coat problems.

If you have allowed your Maltese to become tangled, you may have to cut the hair short with scissors and keep that hair well brushed and free of tangles until the coat grows back.

Growing and maintaining a long coat can be difficult for a novice. On the long, flowing coated breeds there is a minimum of difficult grooming but a maximum of coat work. Puppies should be brushed from two to three times per week. Never brush a dry coat. Always moisten the hair as you brush with an aerosol conditioner or coat dressing to reduce static electricity and prevent coat breakage. Puppies should be bathed every 10 days to two weeks. While the facial hair grows, it often curls into the eyes causing problems that can be easily avoided. The puppy's eyes should be checked and cleaned daily.

If you own a male Maltese and have problems with stained or matted feathering under the body from urine residue, in between shampoos spray the hair with Ring 5 Whitener-Cleaner. Allow the powder to remain on the feathering for about 10 minutes, then brush out completely. Refer to the Chapter on Stained Hair.

Keeping a white Maltese in show condition means a lot of work, especially if the dog is being shown every weekend. As the coat starts getting longer, keep the hair oiled in between shows to encourage growth and prevent breakage. Because coat textures differ, you should experiment a bit to determine the right product for you to use. If you experience difficulties in coat preparations, switch products until you find one that works. To keep the hair oiled, use a light oil in aerosol form, such as Ring 5, Pro-Groom, St. Aubrey Coatasheen or Mr. Groom. For a slightly heavier oil, try Ring 5 Bright & Shine, St. Aubrey Royal Coatalin, Alpha Keri or Lubath (these last two are purchased in a drug store.) The Royal Coatalin comes in a paraffin block form and is applied by first running the pin brush through the block, then through the hair. Royal Coatalin may also be melted on the top of the stove in a pie pan and brushed into the hair in liquid form. The Lubath is poured directly from the bottle onto the coat and brushed through the hair. The Alpha Keri is best applied after the dog has been bathed and rinsed. While the Maltese is still wet, immediately before you remove the dog from the tub, pour the following mixture over the coat. Mix one capful of Alpha Keri with four cups of warm water (you may also add creme rinse to this mixture) and stir the mixture enough to make the oil and water blend. Pour over the coat, squeezing the Alpha Keri mixture through the hair to be sure all areas are saturated. Rinse lightly, take the dog out of the tub and dry as usual. Remember that when you show your Maltese, it must be bathed before the show and no oil of any type rinsed into the coat.

Never over-oil the hair. This only clogs the pores and slows down the hair growth. When keeping a show dog in any oil preparation, it is best to bathe every two weeks to prevent excessive dirt build up caused by oil on the hair.

During the change from puppy to adult coat, you must brush the hair every day to prevent coat loss. To make brushing easier during the coat change, spray the hair with a coat dressing, set your dryer on "Cool" and allow it to blow on the coat as you brush in layers.

As soon as the topknot is long enough, it should be wrapped to encourage growth and prevent breakage. In between shows, the body coat and ear feathering may also be wrapped to protect the ends of the hair and prevent damage. Instructions and photographs are found in "Wrapping The Show Coat."

Before the Show

The Maltese usually requires a bath before the show. The best time to bathe the dog is the evening before exhibition. Once the coat is dry, it is important that you keep the hair on the underbody, legs and feet from becoming dirty or stained. Always confine the dog (cage or exercise pen) in an area covered with white paper or white towels. Never use newspaper! The ink used for printing newspapers is usually the cheapest kind, mainly oil with lampblack. Putting a clean white dog on newspaper will usually result in inkstains on the hair. Most exhibitors prefer using the type of white paper used in physicians' offices to cover examination tables. This kind of paper comes on rolls and can be purchased at any medical supply house.

On the day of the show, spray the coat with Ring 5 Whitener-Cleaner. If the beard area is stained, cover the eyes with your hand and spray Whitener-Cleaner onto the beard. Allow the powder to remain in the coat for about 15 minutes, then brush thoroughly, removing all traces of the Whitener-Cleaner. If the nose is white from the powder, dab a little vaseline onto it, then tissue off. Any stained areas around the eyes can be touched up with EyeTek before the dog goes into the ring.

The Miniature Pinscher

Description of Coat

The Breed Standard describes the coat as "Smooth, hard and short, straight and lustrous, closely adhering to and uniformly covering the body. Faults-Thin, too long, dull; upstanding; curly; dry; area of various thickness or bald spots."

Care of the Pet Dog

The Miniature Pinscher requires a minimum of difficult grooming. Pets should be brushed regularly with a fine-quality bristle brush. Use a medium-soft bristle that will not scratch the dog, but will get into the skin to remove any dirt or dandruff. Brushing a short-haired dog regularly removes the dead hair and keeps the skin clean and the coat glossy. Follow instructions for "Short Haired Dogs" found in the Brushing Chapter.

Periodically, the nails should be cut, the teeth and ears cleaned, whiskers trimmed and anal glands attended to. If groomed regularly, a Miniature Pinscher rarely needs a bath. An occasional wipe-down with a terry towel moistened with Coat Dressing or a Dri-Bath shampoo will keep the coat clean. When a bath is necessary, follow instructions found in the Bathing Chapter.

Care of the Show Dog

If you intend to show your Miniature Pinscher, there are a few additional steps to follow to prepare the dog for the ring. This additional grooming will take only a short time a day or two before the show. Follow this step-by-step procedure:

1. Bathe the dog, if necessary. Shampoo with a tearless protein shampoo and be sure to rinse well.
2. When the dog is dry, place him on the grooming table. If necessary, use clippers with a #10 blade to remove any excess hair from the stomach area. Stand the dog up on his hind legs, point clippers upward and clip from above the genitals to the middle of the dog.
3. Stand the dog on the table with hindquarters facing you for the finishing touches, which will be done with thinning shears and blunt-edged scissors. The Miniature Pinscher should have a sleek, sculptured outline and now you should go over the dog from head to tail, trimming off any hairs that stick out to spoil

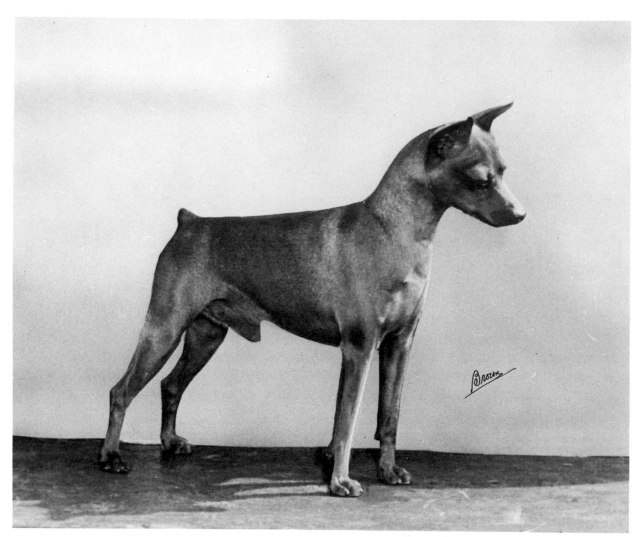

Photograph 127. The Miniature Pinscher is an active, alert smooth-coated breed that was developed in Germany and has gained popularity all over the world. His smooth coat makes him easy to look after with regular brushing and just some judicious trimming for appearances in the show ring.

this outline. *Remember, you are not trying to see how much hair you can scissor off, so don't overtrim and make bare spots. There will be very little scissoring necessary!* Start by removing all straggly hairs from the pads underneath the back feet. Thin any shaggy ridges on the hindquarters near the tail. Neaten any uneven hairs on the tail or at the end of the tail. Check the rest of the body, especially the tuck-up and brisket and thin any hairs that stick out and spoil the sleek outline.

4. Turn the dog around to stand facing you. Remove any uneven hairs from the feet and pads underneath the toes on the front legs. Check the elbows, front of chest and shoulders for straggly hairs that spoil the sleek outline.
5. Do the head last. With blunt-edged scissors, remove the whiskers. Thin any shaggy tufts of hair at the base of the ear.

Before going into the show ring, spray the coat with Ring 5 Bright & Shine to deepen the coat color and polish with the rubber brush described in the Equipment Chapter.

Photograph 127 shows the finished Miniature Pinscher.

The Papillon

An elegant, fine-boned toy dog, the Papillon's large ears resemble the spread wings of a butterfly. In fact, the breed takes its name from the French world *papillon,* meaning butterfly.

Description of Coat

The Breed Standard describes the coat as "abundant, long, fine, silky, flowing, straight with resilient quality, flat on back and sides of body. A profuse frill is on chest. There is no undercoat. Hair short and close on skull, muzzle, front of forelegs and from hind feet to hocks. Ears well fringed with the inside covered with silken hair of medium length. Backs of the forelegs are covered with feathers diminishing to the pasterns. Hindlegs are covered to the hocks with abundant breeches (culottes). Tail is covered with a long flowing plume. Hair on feet is short but fine tufts may appear over toes and grow beyond them forming a point.

Brushing and Combing

The Papillon should be brushed with a small-sized pin brush or natural bristle brush. If the coat is matted, use the small size Twinco slicker brush. Stand the dog on the grooming table with the hindquarters facing you. Spray the coat with an aerosol conditioner. Begin brushing the back legs first. These should be covered to the hock joints with profuse feathers, also called "breeches" and it is best to brush this long hair in layers, using a downward stroke of the brush. Always begin near the hock joint and work upward, lifting up the long breeching above the area you are brushing with your free hand to separate it from the layer you are brushing. Next, brush out the tail plume. Then brush the body coat, first stroking against the growth of hair and finishing by brushing from neck to tail. Turn the dog around to stand facing you. Brush the frill around the neck and the hair on the front of the chest. Gently draw each front leg forward to brush out the feathering on the back of each foreleg. Brush the ear fringes downward.

Use a metal comb with teeth long enough to get through the long hair. Comb through the coat to be sure all mats are removed.

Pre-Bath Preparations

Clean ears, cut nails and check anal glands.

Bathing and Drying

If the Papillon is brushed and combed properly, it will seldom need a bath. The resilient quality of the coat described in the Standard enables the hair to easily shed dirt. However, the show Papillon should be bathed one or two days before the show. Follow instructions found in the Bathing Chapter. Give two shampoos, using a whitener shampoo on the body and legs and a tearless preparation on the head. Rinse well and follow with a creme rinse. Fluff dry the dog, brushing the coat as instructed above.

Finishing

Stand the dog on the grooming table. Lift each back foot and cut out the excessive hair between the pads underneath. Then put each foot down on the grooming table in a normal standing position and scissor the sides of the foot only, not the hair near the toenails. The standard calls for thin and elongated feet with hair growing between the toes, forming a point.

Use thinning shears to tidy any long hair from below the hock joint to the foot. On a pet, any unruly body or breeching hair may be thinned with thinning shears, but this should not be done to the show Papillon. The long whiskers on the face and above the eyes may be scissored off. The underside of the front feet should be trimmed of excess hair. Then with the foot in a standing position, scissor the sides only, not the hair near the toenails.

To finish, brush the body coat flat on the back and sides. Brush the breechings on the hind leg outward and downward. Brush the chest frill upward and outward to fluff up the collarette. Brush the tail in the opposite direction to make the plume appear profuse. Brush the ear fringes outward to enhance the butterfly appearance.

Photograph 128 shows the finished Papillon.

General Suggestions for Coat Care

In between shows, a protein aerosol conditioner is best for maintaining the coat. This preparation should be used on the hair several times a week, as the coat is brushed. Because the Papillon has no undercoat, shedding is slight.

For show dogs, about an hour before the dog goes into the ring, spray all white parts of the coat with Ring 5 Whitener-Cleaner. Brush the hair as directed above, making sure all traces of the powder are out of the coat before the dog goes into the ring.

Photograph 128. The Papillon is a breed of natural beauty. Aside from regular grooming, he requires only the tidying of feet and trimming of the facial feelers.

The Pekingese

Description of Coat

The Breed Standard describes the coat as "long, with thick undercoat, straight and flat, not curly nor wavy, rather coarse but soft; feather on thighs, legs, tail and toes long and profuse. Mane—profuse, extending beyond the shoulder blades, forming a ruff or frill around the neck."

Necessary Grooming Equipment

The correct brush for the Pekingese is a natural bristle or pin brush. Each brush type is described in the Equipment Chapter. When selecting a pin brush for the show Peke, buy one with long, flexible brass or stainless steel pins to prevent coat damage. A soft toothbrush is necessary for cleaning and brushing the facial wrinkle. You also need the half-fine, half-medium combination comb described in the Equipment Chapter. The comb is used sparingly on the feathering and the brush on the long body coat, chest and mane.

General Cleaning

If the hair is brushed properly at least three times a week, the Peke rarely needs a bath. Show dogs are seldom bathed as shampoo and water soften and flatten the coat. If it is necessary to bathe a show Peke, shampoo *at least two weeks before the show* with a texturizer shampoo to allow the coarse texture to return to the hair. It is necessary, however, to clean the coat regularly. Since the Pekingese is a heavy coated, low-to-the ground breed, the legs and underbody areas attract dirt and often become grimy quickly. This needs regular cleaning to prevent urine staining or dirty long skirt feathering, both of which cause unpleasant odors and weaken and damage the hair shafts. Rather than bathing, the long underbody feathering, legs and feet should be sponged off from two to three times per week without wetting the entire dog. Sponge the hair with warm water then blot the coat dry with a towel. Dust some Ring 5 Whitener-Cleaner or silicone grooming powder into the damp hair and brush the coat dry as usual. You may also use any of the Dri-Bath methods mentioned in the Bathing Chapter to clean the long coat.

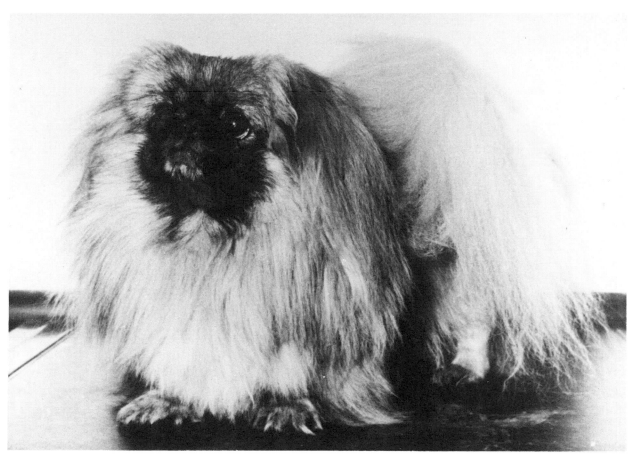

Photograph 129. The stately Pekingese was for centuries a favored pet of Chinese rulers. Today he makes his regal presence felt in the home and the show ring. His coat, which is one of his hallmarks, is not difficult to keep in order if the dog is regularly brushed.

Care of the Eyes

The Pekingese has large eyes set in shallow sockets which can be easily scratched and infected since this type of eye is more prominent and not as protected as a smaller eye. Be sure to read the Eye Care Chapter carefully and check the eyes daily for irritation.

Care of the Facial Wrinkle

After cleaning the Peke's eyes, press the wrinkle away from the eyeball and wash with lukewarm water and the soft toothbrush mentioned before. Use a cotton ball or tissue to dry the wrinkle. This should be done daily to prevent soreness and irritation. After the wrinkle has been dried, dip a Q-Tip in silicone grooming powder or cornstarch and rub over the wrinkle to keep the area dry.

Miscellaneous Care

The Pekingese has drop ears which need regular attention. Wax and dirt can accumulate inside and cause problems. Follow directions in the Ear Cleaning Chapter. Nails should be trimmed short following instructions in the Nail Care Chapter. Anal Glands and teeth should be checked monthly.

Trimming the Feet

The hair in between the pads on the underside of each foot may be scissored. On the tops of the feet, do not scissor away any hair. As mentioned in the Breed Standard, the feathering on the toes should be long and profuse.

Brushing

Begin by brushing the hair under the chest. On a Pekingese, the easiest way to do this is to sit in a chair, spreading a towel over your legs. Place the dog on its back in your lap. Many pets are not accustomed to this brushing method and may squirm when you first turn them over but, by holding the dog gently and speaking quietly and reassuringly, the dog will eventually relax.

Begin at the stomach and work up to the chest, parting the hair in layers and brushing downward from the skin out to the ends of the coat. Spray each layer of hair with a fine mist of aerosol coat conditioner or coat dressing, then place your brush near the skin and brush with a light sweeping stroke that goes beyond the ends of each layer to prevent hair breakage. While the dog is in this position, brush the hair on the insides of the back legs and the hard-to-get areas under the front legs. When you have brushed all the underbody hair, begin again at the front of the chest and brush the hair upward and forward in the same layering method. Photographs showing layer brushing are included in the Brushing Chapter at the front of this book.

The rest of the body coat is brushed with the dog lying on its side on the grooming table. Beginning at the hindquarters, part and brush the hair in layers as you work toward the head. Before brushing, moisten each layer with a protein aerosol coat conditioner, coat dressing or distilled water to prevent static electricity. Brush downward with gentle, slow strokes that sweep beyond the ends of the hair to prevent damage. As you brush, separate any mats in the hair with your fingers, then

Diagram 14. Refer to this chart for properly brushing the Pekingese. The direction of the arrows indicate how the coat should be brushed to achieve the breed's "lion-like" appearance.

gently work them out with the brush. Keep working toward the head. Double-check the hair behind the ears and be sure to remove all tangles. Turn the dog over and brush the other side of the body in the same manner.

When both sides of the dog have been layer brushed to the skin and all mats and tangles removed, stand the dog on the grooming table and finish brushing the hair into proper position as indicated on Diagram 14:

1. The body hair behind the mane to the base of the tail is brushed backward.
2. Brush the hair on each side of the body outward to emphasize rib spring.
3. Brush the breechings downward to emphasize length, then forward to emphasize profuseness.
4. Brush the tail forward, letting the plume fall over each side of the body. In most cases when brushed forward, the tail plume covers the body coat all the way to the head.
5. Brush the mane forward towards the head.
6. Brush the ruff or frill under the chin upward and outward to emphasize the broadness of chest.
7. The Pekingese has a large head with a flat, wide topskull and broad muzzle. The hair on the skull is brushed flat. There should be no dome-head look. The hair on the sides of the head and cheeks is brushed forward to create a frame around the face, emphasizing the massive and broad skull.
8. Brush the ear feathering downward and forward.

Photograph 129 shows the finished Pekingese.

Grooming the Pet Pekingese

As previously stated, the Pekingese coat requires regular brushing. A well-brushed coat is naturally oily, looks healthier and more glossy than unbrushed hair. However, some pet owners never try to establish a regular grooming routine, consequently the tail plume, long skirt feathering and rest of the coat become dirty and matted.

Although trimming is not recommended for the Pekingese, in some cases of neglect, it is better if the pet's coat is shortened for easy maintenance. The hair should not be clipped off. Instead, to maintain the overall beauty of the correct Peke type, the coat may be shortened by using the following method:

1. Brush the coat. Use a tangle remover if the pet is matted.
2. Bathe the dog if the coat is dirty following directions in the Bathing Chapter. A creme rinse will soften the coat but is recommended for neglected pets to help keep the coat more manageable between groomings. Brush the coat dry as instructed in the Bathing Chapter.
3. When the coat is completely dry, stand the dog on the grooming table. Use thinning shears to thin out the hair. As directed in the Equipment Chapter, hold the thinning shears close to the skin in a vertical position. Doing this helps to remove the excess bulk without shortening the hair length.
4. If a shorter coat is desired, use regular scissors to shorten the length. Work on small sections at a time, gradually blending and tapering the ends of the hair, rather than blunt-cutting large areas.

Suggestions for Coat Maintenance

While the puppy coat is growing and for adult maintenance, the hair should be brushed thoroughly about three times a week to keep the coat clean. Before brushing, lightly spray the coat with an aerosol protein conditioner, coat dressing or distilled water to prevent static electricity and coat breakage.

Remember that the Pekingese has a double-coat. The thick undercoat supports the long outercoat and gives the hair a coarse, stand-out appearance. When brushing, always take care not to pull out too much undercoat. Without undercoat, the Peke's outer coat appears flat and soft and the overall Pekingese type is spoiled. Puppies start to shed at about four months (although a small amount of shedding goes on all the time). Pekingese shed twice a year, in late spring and early fall. Extra coat care is necessary during the shedding seasons, change from puppy to adult coat and on bitches after whelping a litter of puppies. During these periods, the coat should be brushed thoroughly to remove excessive dead hair and prevent skin problems.

If you experience skin problems, Ring 5 Medicated Spray or a medicated shampoo will help relieve itching, summer-type rashes and other non-specific types of dermatitis.

Extra care is required in the summer months. Never exercise your Peke in direct sunlight as this will fade the coat color. If the dog is exercised outdoors, it should be done in early morning, at sundown or in the shade. Keep the Pekingese as cool and comfortable as possible. At shows, fresh water or ice cubes should be on hand to keep the dog cool.

Be sure to clean the eyes and facial wrinkle daily to prevent soreness and irritation.

In spite of the abundance of coat on the show Pekingese, the hair is not difficult to maintain if a regular grooming routine is established. The hair should be dampened and brushed three times a week. To dampen the coat, use a spray bottle filled with coat dressing, distilled or rain water and brush as directed in the grooming instructions. In between shows, the Peke's coat can be kept in a light oil to prevent matting and tangling. Be sure to keep the ear feathering oiled to protect the ends as the ear feathering should be long to help form a frame around the face. A protein-lanolin aerosol formulation seems best for the Pekingese coat as this type of preparation is not greasy, helps to repair damaged hair and, with regular use, adds body to the coat. There will be less oil build-up with a protein product to attract dirt.

The Day of the Show

About one to 1-1/2 hours before the Pekingese goes into the ring, fill a spray bottle with coat dressing, rain or distilled water. Spray the entire coat with the exception of the head area, lifting the long outercoat so that the liquid moistens the undercoat. Do not overwet the dog; just spray enough to lightly dampen the entire body coat, feathering and tail plume. If you mistakenly wet the coat too much, rub with a terry towel until the right degree of dampness results. Spray Ring 5 Whitener-Cleaner or a silicone grooming powder into the damp hair, again lifting the outercoat to permit the powder to penetrate the undercoat. Return the dog to its cage. About 45 minutes before exhibition, brush the coat as directed in the grooming instructions. Brush until the coat is dry and all traces of powder are removed from the coat. Always remember that the powder is being used as a cleaner, not as a whitener in this case. Dampen a face cloth and lightly wipe over the face. Check the eyes and clean if necessary. Be sure the wrinkle area is dry. If any traces of powder appear on the nose, dab some vaseline or baby oil on the nose and wipe clean with a tissue or cotton ball.

The Pomeranian

Description of Coat

The Breed Standard describes the Pomeranian as "Double-coated; a short, soft, thick undercoat, with longer, coarse, glistening outer coat, consisting of guard hairs which must be harsh to the touch in order to give the proper texture of the coat to form a frill of profuse, standing-off straight hair. The front legs are well feathered and the hindquarters are clad with long hair or feathering from the top of the rump to the hocks." The Standard also states that "trimming for neatness is permissible around the feet and up the back of the legs to the first joint; trimming on unruly hairs on the edges of the ears and around the anus is also permitted."

Necessary Grooming Equipment

The correct brush for the Pomeranian is a natural or nylon bristle or pin brush. Each brush type is described in the Equipment Chapter. Many breeders feel that a pin brush tends to break off the ends of the hair and pull out undercoat. The Pomeranian's coat will not be damaged, however, if you select a pin brush with flexible brass or stainless steel pins.

You also need the half-fine, half-medium combination comb described in the equipment chapter. The comb is used sparingly on the body as it can pull out too much hair, but it is necessary to comb the ears, tail and breechings. The medium side is used for combing the body and the fine side for the head and ears. You also need a pair of regular scissors and a pair of thinning shears.

Brushing

Begin by brushing the hair under the chest. On a toy dog, the easiest way to do this is to sit in a chair, spreading a towel over your legs. Place the dog on its back in your lap. Many pets are not accustomed to this brushing method and may squirm when you first turn them over but, by holding the dog gently and speaking quietly and reassuringly, the dog eventually will relax.

Begin at the stomach and work up to the chest, parting the hair in layers and brushing downward from the skin out to the ends of the coat. Spray each layer of hair with a fine mist of aerosol coat conditioner or coat dressing, then place your brush near the skin and brush with a light sweeping stroke that goes beyond the end of each layer to prevent hair breakage. While the dog is in this position, brush the breechings on the insides of the back legs and the hard-to-get areas under the front legs. When you have brushed all the underbody hair, begin again at the front of the chest and brush the hair upward and forward in the same layering method. Photographs showing layer brushing are included in the Brushing Chapter at the front of this book.

The rest of the body coat is brushed with the dog lying on its side on the grooming table. Have the dog lie with its feet facing you. Beginning at the hindquarters, part and brush the hair in layers as you work toward the head. Before brushing, moisten each layer with coat conditioner or dressing to prevent static electricity. Brush downward with gentle, slow strokes that sweep beyond the ends of the hair to prevent damage. As you brush, separate any mats in the hair with your fingers, then gently work them apart with the brush. Keep working upward in layers toward the head. Always double-check the hair behind the ears, using extra coat conditioner if the hair is matted. Turn the dog over and brush the other side of the body in the same manner.

When both sides of the dog have been layer brushed to the skin and all mats and tangles removed, stand the dog on the table and brush as follows:

Body Coat: upward and forward.

Tail Plume: forward in layers, then let it fall over the back.

Breechings On Back Legs: downward in layers.

Apron Under Chin: upwards.

Neck Ruff: Upwards.

Miscellaneous

Trim the nails, clean the ears and check anal glands before bathing or at least once a month. Check eyes daily and remove accumulated matter in corners.

Bathing

If the coat is brushed properly about three times a week, the Pomeranian rarely needs a bath. On show dogs, bathing seldom is done because shampoo and water soften and flatten the hair. If it is necessary to bathe a show Pom, always shampoo at least two weeks before the show to allow the harsh texture to return to the hair. If the legs or underbody areas are dirty or stained, these parts are easy to clean without wetting the entire dog. For both pets and show dogs, when a bath is necessary, use the Dri-Bath method or follow shampoo directions found in the Bathing Chapter. Use a protein or texturizer shampoo to preserve coat texture, bathe twice and rinse well. Do not use a creme rinse after shampooing. Brush the coat dry in layers as instructed in the Bathing Chapter.

Trimming the Ears

Hold the ear between the thumb and index finger so that the tip is uncovered for trimming. With scissors, make a cut on the outside edge of each ear from the tip downward about ½″ as shown in Sketch A. Do not follow the line of the ear leather, but scissor as the arrows indicate in the sketch. Next, make a cut on the inside edge of each ear from the tip downward about ⅛″ as shown in Sketch B. Notice that the inside cuts are shorter in length than the outside cuts. This creates the impression of

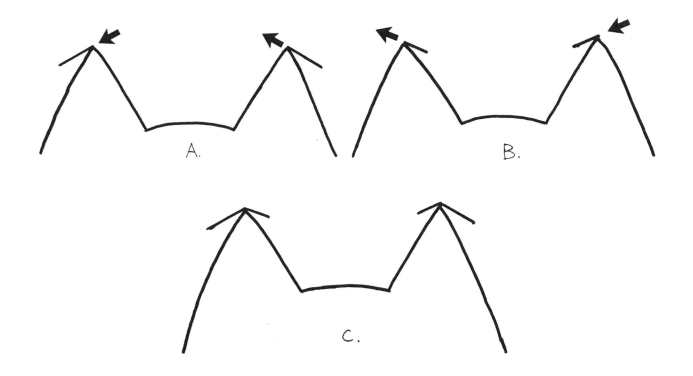

Diagram 15. These sketches illustrate how to trim the Pomeranian's ears so that they conform to the requirements of the Standard.

Diagram 16. These drawings show the "before" and "after" of trimming the Pomeranian's hindlegs. Only the excess hair is removed. The foot shows substance in relation to size but should not appear obviously overtrimmed.

135

small ears. Do not trim the entire ear or you will make it appear too large. The $\frac{1}{2}''$ and $\frac{1}{8}''$ measurements are for medium-sized Pomeranians; smaller dogs will need less scissoring and larger Poms need more hair taken off. On the ear leathers above the scissor lines, use an extra-fine thinning shears to trim the ear tips of straggly hairs.

Trimming the Feet, Back and Front Legs

The feet and lower parts of the back and front legs require trimming. Begin by scissoring all excess hair between the pads underneath each foot. Next, with the foot in a normal standing position, thin any long hairs which stick out from between the toes. Do not overtrim the feet. Only the excess hair is trimmed to make the feet appear neat. The nails should not be exposed.

Each back leg should be trimmed from the foot up to the hock joint. The sides, back and front of each leg are trimmed with extra-fine thinning shears to make them appear neat. Diagram 16 shows the back leg and foot before trimming and shows the same area after thinning. The front and sides of the front legs are thinned in the same manner with the extra-fine thinning shears.

Trimming the Anal Area

The anal area is trimmed to look neat and clean. Scissor away all hairs that cover the anus and could possibly cause clogging problems.

Trimming the Tail

If the tail plume is straggly, the tips at the end of the plume can be scissored. Use the scissors to tip off only the straggly ends of the hairs; do not overscissor.

Trimming the Head

Do not use clippers on the muzzle at any time. Whiskers may be scissored off or left on the face, according to personal preference. Trimming the whiskers helps to refine a coarse muzzle somewhat. If any straggly facial hairs curl into the eye corners, pluck them out to prevent eye irritation. (Plucking instructions found in "Brussels Griffon" Chapter.) The hair on the top and sides of the head should be combed with the fine end of the comb in an upward and outward motion to further enhance the ruff around the neck.

Finishing the Body.

As indicated in Diagram 17, begin at the head and brush the body coat upward and forward in layers as you work down to the hindquarters. Brush the breechings on the back legs outward and downward. Brush the neck ruff upward. Brush the apron under the chin upward and outward. Brush the feathering on the back of the front legs outward and downward.

Any straggly hairs may be tipped with scissors to make the coat appear more profuse. Tipping the hair strengthens the hair shaft and gives the impression of a thicker coat. Do not overscissor, just remove the straggly ends of the coat, if necessary. If the Pom appears long in back, shorten the hair on the top of the back near the tail root to make the back look shorter, then place the tail feathering forward over the back.

Photograph 130 shows the finished Pomeranian.

Diagram 17. The Pomeranian's coat should stand away from the body. Brushing in the direction of the arrows on this chart will help you turn out a well-groomed Pom.

Photograph 130. Although a Toy, the Pomeranian belongs to the family of the northern breeds with the Samoyed and the Siberian Husky. Grooming should accentuate the off-standing coat and other features he shares with his larger cousins.

Suggestions for Coat Maintenance

While the puppy coat is growing and for adult maintenance, the hair should be brushed thoroughly from two to three times per week. Before brushing, always moisten the hair with an aerosol protein conditioner or coat dressing, to prevent static electricity and coat damage. Remember that the Pomeranian has a double-coat. The dense undercoat supports the long guard hair and gives the coat a harsh, stand-out appearance. When brushing, always take care not to pull out the undercoat. Without undercoat, the Pomeranian's outer coat appears flat and soft and the overall beauty of the Pomeranian type is destroyed.

Poms shed twice a year, in late spring and early fall. Extra coat care is necessary during the shedding seasons, change from puppy to adult coat, and on bitches after whelping a litter of puppies. During these periods, the coat may need to be brushed daily to remove excessive dead hair and prevent skin problems. When the shedding period begins, the coat should be brushed daily and all dead hair removed as soon as possible, to encourage the growth of new hair.

If you experience skin problems, Ring 5 Medicated Spray or a medicated shampoo will help relieve itching, summer-type rashes and other non-specific types of dermatitis.

In spite of the abundance of coat on the show Pomeranian, the hair is fairly easy to maintain. In between shows, the Pom can be kept in light oil to keep the coat from matting. An aerosol protein-lanolin formulation is best as this type of preparation is not too greasy and repairs any damaged hairs. With regular use, protein products add body to the coat.

During the summer months, do not exercise your Pom in direct sunlight as this will affect the coat color by fading the golds and giving the blacks a reddish cast. Always exercise the dog in the shade, in the early morning or at sundown.

In the summer, many Pomeranians suffer from clogging of the ear tips. If this happens, do not try to pull off the crust that has formed as this will make the ear bleed. Soften the crust with Baby Oil to make it easy to remove. Clean and dry the ear, then massage the tips with Cortisynth Cream to promote healing.

Before the Show

On the day of the show, brush the hair as described in the grooming instructions. Spray the hair with a light mist of coat dressing. Do not saturate the hair; wet the coat just enough to lightly moisten. Rub the coat with a terry towel, then brush upward and forward as sketched to lift the coat into proper position.

The Poodle (Toy)

No other breed can be groomed in as many different coat styles as the Toy, Miniature or Standard Poodle. There are three acceptable clips for the show ring: Continental, English Saddle and Puppy. Both the Continental and English Saddle Clips have a long, lion-like mane over the shoulders, ribs and chest with closely trimmed hindquarters. A young Poodle may be shown in Puppy trim until 12 months of age and then must be clipped in either of the two other recognized styles.

For the pet Poodle, there are a variety of trims, such as the Kennel, Lamb, Summer, Dutch, New Yorker etc., in which the coat is clipped and scissored into various body patterns and leg styles. These clips are called "pet" trims because they are unacceptable in the conformation show ring.

Before describing some of the Poodle coat styles, it is necessary to learn basic Poodle grooming: how to brush the coat, the correct way to bathe the dog and how to clip the face, feet and tail.

Brushing

The easiest way to keep the Poodle's coat in good condition is to brush regularly. Brushing stimulates the growth of new hair; removes dead hair before it has a chance to mat near the skin; keeps the skin clean and makes the Poodle less susceptible to skin disease and parasites. Two different types of brushes are necessary for Poodle hair. The slicker brush described in the Equipment Chapter is correct for any of the pet trims. Instructions for brushing pet Poodles are found in the Brushing Chapter in the front of this book.

For the show coat, a pin brush (also described in the Equipment Chapter) is used on the long mane coat, and a slicker brush on the short hair of the hindquarters, the bracelets or tail. The first step in brushing the show coat is to teach the Poodle to lie on the grooming table while being brushed. Place the dog on his side with feet facing you. The puppy coat or long mane coat (also called the *ruff*) of the English Saddle or Continental styles is brushed in layers. (This method is described in detail in the Brushing Chapter.) Begin by parting the hair lengthwise from the shoulder to the back leg. After the hair is separated, spray the part plus the hair above and below it with a dressing or aerosol conditioner to prevent breakage and static electricity. Place your brush on the part line and brush that section of hair, as shown in Photograph 131. Now make another part lengthwise about one inch below the hair you just brushed and spray and brush that section. Keep parting the hair in layers and brushing down to the chest. Turn the Poodle over and use this same method to brush the other side. Stand the Poodle on the table to brush the hindquarters, bracelets and tail.

Bathing

For pet Poodles, follow directions found in the Bathing Chapter. Give two shampoos and rinse well. If the shampoo you use does not contain extra conditioners, follow with a creme rinse to help make the hair more manageable after the bath. Fluff dry the hair with a slicker brush, using light strokes to lift the hair rather than flatten it.

Before bathing a show Poodle, part the long mane coat down the center of the back, letting the ruff fall to either side of the body. Then follow bathing and drying instructions found in the ''Bathing the Long Show Coat'' section of the Bathing Chapter.

Clipping Face, Feet and Tail

The face is best clipped with the dog in a sitting position, facing you. Beginning on your right side, turn back the ear leather and, using a #10 or #15 blade, clip a straight line from in front of the ear to the corner of the eye. Then clip under the eye. For the best control while you are clipping under the eye, grasp the Poodle's head with the palm of your free hand and use your thumb to stretch the corner of the eye backward. Continue clipping forward on the sides of the face. Press the jaws firmly together when clipping the hair around the lips and nose. Clip the other side of the head the same way. When both sides of the face are clipped, hold the muzzle firmly with your hand and clip a small inverted ''V'' in the space between the inside corners of the eyes. Then lift up the head and clip the hair on the throat and front of the neck.

To clip the feet, place the dog in a sitting position facing you. Begin clipping the back feet first. Use your free hand to pull the back foot forward, close to the front leg. With a

Photograph 131. It is best for the Poodle to lie quietly on its side while being brushed. This will be less wearing on dog and groomer. Such training should and can be done during early puppyhood.

#15 blade, point clippers upward, start near the nails and clip off all the hair on the top of the foot. Clip up only to the end of the foot, stopping at the spot where the foot joins the ankle. Before clipping the hair between the toes, spread the foot by placing the second finger of your free hand in between the large pad and small toe pads on the underside of the foot. At the same time, use your thumb to spread the toes on the top of the foot. Now clip in between the toes with the edge of the clipper blade. Clip the back of the ankle, making sure that the clipped line evenly encircles the foot. Then spread the toes apart on the underside of the foot and clip the excess hair between the pads. All four feet can be clipped with the dog in this position.

To clip the tail, stand the Poodle on the grooming table with hindquarters facing you. Grasp the end of the tail in your free hand and, using clippers with a #10 blade, start at about the middle of the tail stump and clip the top and sides into where the tail joins the body. The underside of this tail is a delicate area and should be clipped in the opposite direction, from the body out to the middle of the tail. The remaining hair is shaped with scissors into a round pompon.

The face, feet and tail are always clipped in this same manner. A moustache is optional when clipping the face of a pet Poodle.

One word of caution: the Poodle's face and tail are sensitive spots and clipping closely may result in clipper rash. White and light-colored Poodles seem to be the most sensitive. Before clipping your Poodle for the first time, refer to the Clipper Burn Chapter for suggestions for sensitive Poodles.

The Puppy Clip

The Poodle may be shown in the conformation ring in Puppy clip until he is one year old. The face, throat, feet and tail are clipped. The rest of the hair is left long on the back, ribs and chest to prepare the coat for the Continental or English Saddle Clip when the Poodle is one year old. The Poodle standard states that "in order to give a neat appearance, a slight shaping of the coat is permissible; however, a Poodle in 'Puppy' clip that is excessively scissored shall be dismissed." Therefore, on the show Puppy clip, very little hair is scissored off the body, with the exception of the hindquarters which are shaped slightly. As the Poodle's mane coat grows long, the ends tend to become straggly. The tops of these uneven ends should be scissored off every four to six weeks to keep the coat in shape and strengthen the hair. This type of scissor work is called "tipping" and does not affect the length of the coat.

The Continental Clip

The face, throat, feet, and tail are clipped. The hindquarters are clipped close, with a pompon (optional) left on each hip. The hip pompons are clipped round and scissored in proportion to the Poodle's size. The back legs are clipped close, leaving hair to be scissored into a bracelet covering each hock. The forelegs are clipped close, leaving enough hair to scissor a puff on each front leg. The long mane coat is left full and shaped round with scissors to emphasize over-all balance. The topknot may be held up with a latex band or barrette.

The English Saddle Clip

The face, throat, feet and tail are clipped. The forelegs are clipped close, leaving enough hair at the bottom of each leg to scissor into a round puff. The hindquarters are covered with a short blanket of hair with a curved, clipped area on each flank called the

Photograph 132. The Kennel Clip has been growing in popularity as it is a good looking clip and is not difficult to keep up. With the exception of the length of the body coat it is the same as the Puppy Clip.

Photograph 133. The English Saddle Clip is the most popular of the three approved show clips for Poodles. The others being the Puppy Clip (for dogs under a year) and the Continental Clip. In the Continental Clip the rear is shaved with the exception of a pompon on the tail, bracelets on the hind legs and pompons (optional) on the hips. The forepart of the dog is clipped the same as in the English Saddle Clip. *Shafer.*

Photograph 134. The Summer, or Miami, Clip is fairly new and developed out of the desire for a clip that was attractive and yet permitted the dog to carry less than the usual amount of coat in warm weather.

Photograph 135. The Dutch Clip is one of the older pet clips. From it has developed dozens of unique, attractive clips to suit the fancy of any Poodle owner.

kidney patch. There are two shaved bands on each back leg. These bands can be made first with scissors and then clipped to avoid making mistakes. The first band is made across the leg at the stifle joint and the second band is clipped at the hock joint. The hair between the clipped bands is shaped with scissors into pompons. The long mane coat is left full and shaped round with scissors to emphasize overall balance. The topknot is held up with a latex band or barrette.

The Kennel and Lamb Clips

Both styles are easy to maintain on a pet Poodle. The face, throat, feet, stomach and tail are clipped. The back of the neck and body are clipped with a #4 or #5 blade to a length of from 1/2″ to 3/4″, leaving a short blanket of curly hair. On the Lamb Clip, the leg hair is scissored to a length of about 3/4″ following the natural angulation, creating an overall Lamb look. On the Kennel Clip, the legs are left fuller and scissored into a modified "pantaloon shape."

The Summer or Miami Clip

An excellent style for warm climates, the Summer Clip is also suggested when a matted Poodle must be clipped short. The face, throat, feet, stomach and tail are clipped. The back of the neck and body are clipped short with a #7 or #5 blade to a length of from 1/4″ to 1/2″. The front and back legs are clipped short with the same blade, leaving puffs of hair to cover the hock joints on the back legs and the ankles on the front legs. The four puffs should be scissored round and be even in size and shape. The topknot is scissored round.

The Dutch Clip

The face, neck, stomach, feet and tail are clipped. The Dutch pattern has a narrow band clipped down the middle of the back from neck to tail, plus circular cuts over the sides of the dog between the ribs and back legs. The hair on the hindquarters and back legs is shaped with scissors into a pantaloon. The hair on the ribs, shoulders and front of chest is scissored round, blending into front legs which are shaped into pantaloons. The topknot is scissored round.

The New Yorker Clip

The face, neck, stomach, feet and tail are clipped. The New Yorker pattern has a wide band clipped around the middle of the dog which extends from about an inch or so in front of the hipbones to the middle of the rib cage. The body hair is scissored round, following the natural contours and the leg hair is left full and scissored into a modified pantaloon shape. The topknot is scissored round.

For further information on all aspects of show and pet clipping and grooming for the Poodle, see THE COMPLETE POODLE CLIPPING AND GROOMING BOOK, also by Shirlee Kalstone and published by Howell Book House.

Photograph 136. The Pug originally developed in China and came to America by way of Holland and England. His short coat is easy to keep well-groomed. Show dogs require only light trimming of the longest hairs, in addition to regular brushing, to look their best. *Shafer*

The Pug

Description of Coat

The Breed Standard describes the coat as "Fine, smooth, soft, short and glossy, neither hard nor woolly."

Care of the Pet Dog

The Pug is another short-haired breed which requires a minimum of trimming. The easiest way to keep the coat in good condition is to brush regularly with a fine-quality bristle brush. Use a medium-soft bristle that will not scratch the dog, but will get into the skin and remove any dead hair, dirt and dandruff. Before brushing, spray the coat with an aerosol conditioner to prevent dryness and add a shine to the hair. Be careful not to use the spray near the Pug's prominent eyes. Use the brush first against the growth of the hair, from the tail to the head, to take out as much dead hair as possible, then brush in the opposite direction, from the head to the tail and down the legs, to smooth the coat.

Do not use the brush on the head area. Because the Pug has large eyes set in shallow sockets, the bristles could easily scratch and irritate the eyes. Clean the head with a soft cloth and be sure to smooth out the facial wrinkles to clean any dirt accumulated there. Since the Pug's eyes are prominent, they should be examined daily and kept free of mucous. Be sure to read the directions in the Eye Care Chapter for the correct way to do this job.

About once a month, pet Pugs should have nails cut, ears cleaned, teeth and anal glands checked and whiskers trimmed. A short-haired dog seldom needs a bath if groomed regularly. An occasional rubdown with a damp sponge or terry towel moistened with Coat Dressing or a Dri-Bath Shampoo will keep the coat clean. When bathing is necessary, follow instructions found in the Bathing Chapter. Because of the Pug's protruding eyes, always use a tearless shampoo on the head area. Wipe the head area with a face cloth, pressing the wrinkle away from the eyes to clean in between the folds. Be sure to rinse all traces of shampoo from the wrinkle. When drying the head, press the wrinkle away from the eyes again, taking a soft tissue or cloth to wipe the folds dry to prevent irritation.

Care of the Show Dog

If you intend to show your Pug, there are a few additional steps to follow to prepare for the show ring. This additional grooming will take only a few minutes and should be done a day or two before the show.

As is the case with all short-haired breeds, the most important factor comes from within. Feeding your dog properly, plus regular conditioning, is the basis for a healthy, shining coat. The show Pug should be brushed daily with the medium-soft bristle brush mentioned before.

Follow this step-by-step procedure:

1. Bathe, if necessary, using a Protein tearless shampoo.
2. When the dog is dry, place him on the grooming table. If necessary, use clippers with a #10 blade to remove any excess hair from the stomach area. Stand the dog up on his hind legs, point clippers upward and clip from above the genitals to the middle of the dog, stopping at the last rib.
3. Stand the dog on the grooming table with hindquarters facing you for the finishing touches, which should be done with thinning shears and blunt-edged scissors. The Pug should have a sleek outline and now you want to go over the dog from head to tail and thin any hairs that stick out to spoil this sleek look by making the dog appear untidy. *Remember, you are not trying to see how much hair you can scissor off, so don't overtrim and make bare spots! There should be very little thinning necessary.*

   Start with the blunt-edged scissors and remove any uneven hairs from the pads underneath the toes. If there are untidy hairs on the backs of the hind legs from the hock to the foot, use thinning shears to take them out. Thin any shaggy ridges on the hindquarters near the tail. Check the rest of the body, especially the tuck-up, brisket and hindquarters and only scissor off any hairs that stick out and make the dog look untidy.
4. Turn the dog around to stand facing you. Remove any uneven hairs from the feet and pads underneath the toes on the front legs. Check the elbows, front of the chest and shoulders and thin any hairs that spoil the sleek outline.
5. Do the head area last. With blunt-edged scissors, remove the whiskers. If there are shaggy tufts of hair at the base of each ear, thin them a little so they appear neat.

Before going into the ring, spray the Pug with Ring 5 Bright & Shine, and brush the coat with the rubber brush described in the Equipment Chapter.

Photograph 136 shows the finished Pug.

The Shih Tzu

Description of Coat

The Breed Standard states that the Shih Tzu should have "a luxurious, long, dense coat. May be slightly wavy but never curly. Good woolly undercoat. The hair on top of the head may be tied up." The legs are short, straight, well-boned, muscular and heavily coated. Legs and feet look massive on account of the wealth of hair. The hair should fall over the eyes and there should be ample whiskers and beard, with the hair on the nose growing upward to create a lovely chrysanthemum-like effect. The beautiful flowing coat of the Shih Tzu is the hallmark of the breed. All colors of Shih Tzu are permitted and coat texture varies somewhat with color.

Brushing and Combing

The correct brush is a natural bristle or pin brush for show coats. On matted pets, you may need to use the small size slicker brush. Since any type of wire brush with bent wire teeth can break off the ends of the long hair, always brush with a light stroke when using a slicker on a matted pet.

The correct comb is the half-fine and half-medium style described in the Equipment Chapter. You will also need a fine-tooth comb with handle for the beard and face.

Before brushing, if the beard area is caked with food, discolored or matted, rub a little tangle remover into the coat. While you brush the rest of the dog, the liquid detangler will loosen any foreign matter caked in the hair, making the beard easier to brush out.

Begin by brushing the hair under the chest. Photographs and instructions for brushing the Shih Tzu in the layering method are found in the "Long, Flowing Coated Breeds" section of the Brushing Chapter.

Brushing the Head

After the body hair has been brushed, sit the dog on the grooming table to brush the head. Brush the hair on the top of the head away from the eyes, as shown in Photograph 137. Brush the hair on the sides of the head and around the mouth, taking care not to injure the eyes with the bristles or pins on the brush. Brush the ear feathering downward.

Photograph 137. Start grooming the Shih Tzu by thoroughly brushing out the hair on top of the head and away from the eyes.

Combing

Once the hair has been thoroughly brushed, comb through the coat with the medium-tooth side to be sure all mats have been removed. A fine-tooth comb is the tool of choice for removing accumulated matter near the eye corners. On matted pets, if you soaked the beard hair in a liquid tangle-remover before starting to brush, this area should comb out easily, with no hair loss.

Eye Care

Shih Tzu have large, rather prominent eyes which should be checked daily and cleaned of any foreign matter. Refer to the Eye Care Chapter.

Pre-Bath Preparations

Clean ears, cut toenails and check anal glands.

Bathing and Drying

Before putting the dog into the water, use the edge of the comb or a knitting needle to part the hair down the center of the back from the top of the head to the tail, letting the long coat fall to each side. Follow directions found in the Bathing Chapter for long, flowing coated breeds. Give two shampoos. Use a whitener shampoo on bi-colored Shih Tzu and a protein shampoo on all other colors. Wash the eye area with a tearless shampoo. When washing the body, always keep the part in the center of the back to prevent tangling. If the beard and hair under the eyes are badly stained, dip a toothbrush into the shampoo and gently scrub these areas. Rinse all traces of soap out of the coat. Do use a creme rinse to make the hair more manageable after bathing. Select a brand that has been formulated to make the coat hang straight. Always brush the coat dry, following directions in the Bathing Chapter. While the dryer blows on the wet hair, keep the part in the center of the back as you brush each side downward in the direction that the hair grows.

Finishing the Shih Tzu

STOMACH: This step in Shih Tzu grooming is optional and a matter of personal preference. To keep the genital area clean and prevent hair staining, clip the area with a #10 or #15 blade. Clip off only a little hair. Be careful not to cut off any long feathering under the chest.

FEET: Scissor the hair from between the pads underneath each foot, as shown in Photograph 138. Then place the foot down in a normal standing position. Holding up any long leg hair with your free hand, comb the hair on the foot, fanning the coat out in a large circle. Scissor off any straggly hairs which detract from the round shape. Do not over-scissor around the feet as they should be massive looking with an abundance of hair.

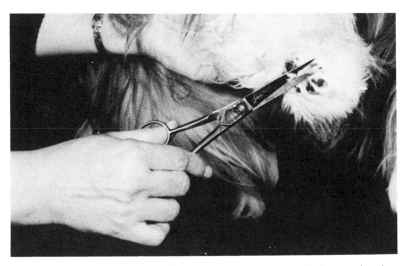

Photograph 138. Use the scissor to remove excess hair growing between the footpads. This will make for neater and cleaner feet.

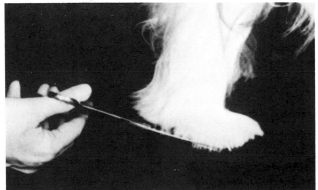

Photograph 139. After scissoring the pads, scissor the outside of the foot to roundness. But take care not to overdo. A barbered look in a Shih Tzu is highly undesirable.

149

BODY: Use the edge of the comb or a knitting needle, as shown in Photograph 140 to part the hair down the center of the back from the top of the head to the base of the tail. Brush the long hair on each side of the part straight down. When the part is straight, spray the back with a light mist of coat dressing, aerosol protein conditioner or the "dry type" hair spray made for men. Comb the hair on the front of the chest downward. On the pet Shih Tzu only, if there are untidy hairs near the tail, these must never be scissored or clipped off, but may be thinned with thinning shears, to make this area look neat.

TAIL: Brush the tail forward, letting the long feathering fall over the back.

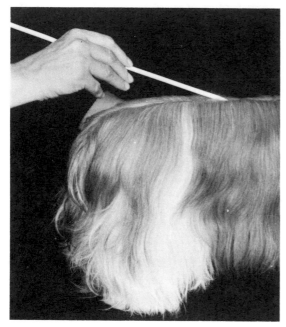

Photograph 140. The Shih Tzu's coat should have a straight part from the back of the neck to the base of the tail. To make this as straight as possible, many people will use a knitting needle to set the hairs where desired.

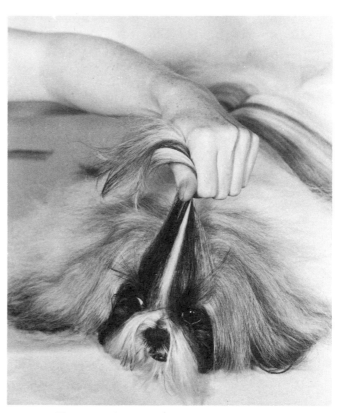

Photograph 141. The hair for the topknot should be parted on a line from about the middle of each eye. This will vary somewhat with the individual, depending on overall expression.

HEAD: One of the distinguishing features of the Shih Tzu is the way in which the topknot is tied up. As shown in Photograph 141, the hair is parted from about the middle of each eye, straight up to the top of the head. Then a part is made across the top of the head, as shown in Photograph 142. Make sure the part is even on both sides. Pull the topknot straight back and fasten with a latex band, as shown in Photograph 143. Use a band small enough to turn only twice. Too much pressure from a heavy rubber band can cause hair breakage, so always try to use a latex orthodontal-type band for the topknot. As shown in Photograph 144, puff up the topknot directly above the eyes with your fingers or a knitting needle. If any wispy hairs slip out from the band above the eyes, use a light touch of hair styling gel to hold them in place. The topknot is then divided in half, and fanned out on each side of the head, as shown in Photograph 145, to resemble a palm tree. Brush the ear

150

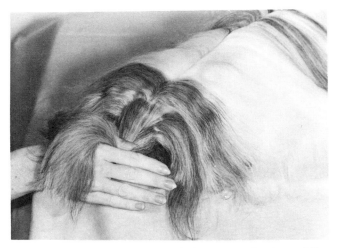

Photograph 142. Parting the hair across the top of the head to make the Shih Tzu's topknot.

Photograph 143. The topknot should be secured with a small latex band. Care should be taken that the topknot is not pulled too tight.

feathering downward. The facial furnishings are parted over the nose and combed to each side of the mouth, creating a mandarin effect. The arrows in the photograph show the correct combing direction to create the mandarin effect. Photograph 146 shows the finished head.

Photograph 147 shows a side view of the finished Shih Tzu.

Suggestions for Coat Care

The Shih Tzu should be brushed regularly at least three times a week. Regular brushing removes the dead hair before it has a chance to mat at the skin. Many Shih Tzu suffer from dry skin which often makes the coat dry and causes scratching. To minimize this condition, an internal skin and coat food supplement such as Linatone may be added to the diet. If the dog is not brushed regularly, the dead hair will mat and cause serious problems. If you have allowed your pet Shih Tzu to become matted, the best thing to do is to scissor the hair off to about two inches in length and try to keep this short coat brushed and conditioned until it grows long again.

Growing and maintaining a long coat can be difficult for a novice. The puppy should be brushed from two to three times a week. Never brush a dry coat, but always moisten the hair with an aerosol protein conditioner or coat dressing before you brush to reduce static electricity and coat breakage. While your puppy is young, get him accustomed to having the hard-to-get spots brushed and combed under the chest, under the front and back legs and on the beard. A puppy should be bathed every ten days to two weeks. The Shih Tzu's eyes are prominent and set in shallow sockets and need daily attention. This is especially true when the puppy hair is short and sometimes curls into the eyes causing problems.

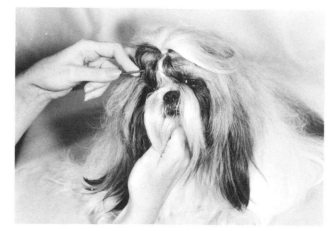

Photograph 144. After securing the topknot, use a knitting needle as shown to puff out the lower section.

Photograph 145. The topknot is parted in the center and fanned out to resemble a palm tree. The hair on the foreface is parted over the muzzle and combed to either side of the mouth. The arrows indicate direction the coat should be.

Photograph 146. Here is the finished Shih Tzu head. Expression is very important in this breed, the dog resembling a tiny mandarin. Correct grooming of the head and face furnishings will help to create this impression on the observer.

Photograph 147. The finished Shih Tzu should resemble this model. The breed should always be strongly reminiscent of its oriental background as well as its imperial history.

Photograph 148. The typical Shih Tzu head should be massive in relation to the dog's overall size. That impression can be heightened if necessary by making the topknot narrower than usual.

Photograph 149. Just as a narrow topknot can help a smallish head, a wider topknot can enhance certain expressions. Study of dogs at shows and various groomers' methods can help you get the most out of your own Shih Tzu.

If you own a male Shih Tzu and have problems with stained or matted feathering under the body from urine residue, spray the hair in between shampoos with Ring 5 Whitener-Cleaner. Allow the powder to remain on the feathering for about 10 minutes, then brush out completely. Refer to the Chapter entitled "How To Treat Stained Hair."

As the Shih Tzu's coat starts getting longer, keep the hair oiled in between shows to encourage growth and prevent hair breakage. Because the coat texture differs with color, you will have to experiment a bit to determine which is the right product to use. Certain textures gum up with the use of one product and respond beautifully to another. If you experience difficulty with one coat preparation, switch products until you find one that works. To keep the hair oiled, use a light oil in aerosol form, such as Ring 5, Pro-Groom, St. Aubrey Coatasheen or Mr. Groom. For a slightly heavier oil, try Ring 5 Bright & Shine, St. Aubrey Royal Coatalin, Alpha Keri or Lubath (these last two are purchased in a drug store). The Royal Coatalin comes in a paraffin block form and is applied by first running the pin brush through the block, then through the hair. Royal Coatalin may also be melted on the top of the stove in a pie pan and brushed into the hair in liquid form. The Lubath is poured directly from the bottle onto the coat and brushed through the hair. The Alpha Keri is best applied after the dog has been bathed and rinsed. While the Shih Tzu is still wet, immediately before you remove him from the tub, pour the following mixture over the coat. Mix one capful of Alpha Keri with four cups of warm water (you may add creme rinse to this mixture) and stir the mixture enough to make the oil and water blend. Pour over the coat, squeezing the Alpha Keri mixture through the hair to be sure all areas are saturated. Rinse lightly, take the dog out of the tub and dry as usual. Remember that when you show your Shih Tzu, he must be bathed before the show and no oil of any type rinsed into the coat.

Never over-oil the hair. This only clogs the pores and slows down the hair growth. When keeping a show dog in any oil preparation, it is best to bathe every two weeks to prevent excessive dirt build-up caused by oil on the hair.

During the change from puppy to adult coat, you must brush the hair every day to prevent coat loss. To make brushing easier during the coat change, spray the hair with a coat dressing or light protein conditioner, set your dryer on "Cool" and allow it to blow on the coat as you brush in layers. Take care, during this transition period of coat change, to protect the undercoat and prevent it from being pulled out by the brush.

As soon as the fall is long enough, it should be wrapped to encourage growth and prevent breakage. In between shows, the long body coat and ear feathering may also be wrapped to protect the ends of the hair and prevent damage. Instructions and photographs are found in "Wrapping The Show Coat."

It is difficult to describe the ideal texture of the Shih Tzu, since texture varies with color. Blue/black is the softest texture and slow to grow. Gunmetal or dark grey is a firm, harsh texture. The lighter shade of grey grows quickly and is firm in texture. The most durable texture is the clear gold color. White, usually combined with black, gold or grey, seems to grow the fastest in the shortest time. With black, the white is the whitest; with gold, the white has a creamy cast and with grey, the white has a grey cast.

During the summer months or in year-round hot climates, never exercise your Shih Tzu in direct sunlight, as this will fade the coat color. Always put the dog outside in the shade, early morning or at sundown.

Before the Show

The Shih Tzu usually requires a bath before the show. The best time to bathe the dog is the evening before exhibition. Once the coat is dry, it is important that you keep the hair on the underbody, legs and feet from becoming dirty or stained. Always confine the dog (cage or exercise pen) in an area covered with white paper or white towels. Never use newspaper! The ink used for printing newspapers is usually the cheapest kind, mainly oil with lampblack. Putting a clean white or light-colored dog on newspaper will usually result in inkstains on the hair. Most exhibitors prefer using the type of white paper used in physicians' offices to cover examination tables. This kind of paper comes on rolls and can be purchased at any medical supply house.

On the day of the show, the coat should be sprayed with a coat dressing which does not contain a heavy oil. All white or light colored areas should be sprayed with Ring 5 Whitener-Cleaner (this product is especially effective for beards). Brush thoroughly to remove all traces of powder from the coat. Any stained areas around the eyes can be touched up with EyeTek before the dog goes into the ring.

The Silky Terrier

Description of Coat

The breed standard describes the ideal coat texture and color as: "Coat—Flat in texture fine, glossy, silky; on mature specimens the desired length of coat from behind the ears to the set-on of the tail is from five to six inches. On top of the head the hair is so profuse as to form a topknot, but long hair on face and ears is objectionable. Legs from knee and hock joints to feet should be free from long hair. The hair is parted on the head and down over the back to the root of the tail. Color—Blue and tan. The blue may be silver blue, pigeon blue or slate blue, the tan deep and rich. The blue extends from the base of the skull to the tip of the tail, down the forelegs to the pasterns, and down the thighs to the hocks. On the tail the blue should be very dark. Tan appears on the muzzle and cheeks, around the base of the ears, below the pasterns and hocks, and around the vent. There is a tan spot over each eye. The topknot should be silver or fawn."

Brushing and Combing

The correct brush for the Silky Terrier is a natural or nylon bristle brush. The correct comb is the half-fine and half-medium style illustrated in the Equipment Chapter. You will also need an extra-fine flea comb for the facial furnishings.

Begin by brushing the hair under the chest. On a toy dog, the easiest way to do this is to sit in a chair, spreading a towel over your legs. Place the dog on its back in your lap. Photographs and instructions for brushing the chest hair in this manner are found in the Brushing Chapter.

The rest of the body coat is brushed in the layering method also described and illustrated in the Brushing Chapter.

Sit the dog on the grooming table while you brush the head. Brush the hair on the top of the head away from the eyes, taking care not to injure the eyes with the brush bristles.

After the hair has been thoroughly brushed, comb through the coat using the medium end of the comb first, then the fine end, to be sure all tangles have been removed. Use the extra-fine flea comb to remove any matter accumulated in the hair near the eyes or around the mouth.

Pre-Bath Preparations

Clean ears, trim toenails and check the anal glands.

Bathing and Drying

Before putting the Silky Terrier into the water, part the hair down the center of the back. Follow instructions found in the Bathing Chapter. Give two shampoos and wash the head area with a tearless shampoo. If the facial hair is stained, dip a toothbrush into the shampoo and gently scrub these areas. Use a creme rinse. Select a brand that has been formulated to make the coat hang straight. Always brush the coat dry. While the dryer blows on the wet hair, keep the part in the center of the back as you brush each side downward in the direction that it grows.

Finishing the Silky Terrier

STOMACH: This step is optional and a matter of personal preference. If you own a pet male Silky Terrier and are troubled with stained or matted hair from urine residue, clip the genital area with a #10 blade.

LEGS AND FEET: The legs from the knee and hock joints to the feet should be free from long hair. The hair should be shortened to a length of from 1/4 to 1/2 inch with a stripping comb or Duplex Dresser. It must never be trimmed close to the skin with a clipper.

Diagram 18 shows the side view of the Silky Terrier prior to leg and foot trimming. Before stripping, comb the hair with the fine-tooth flea comb to remove as much dead hair as possible. The correct stripping technique is to hold the knife or dresser with

Diagram 18. Left to itself the hair below the hocks will grow long and untidy. This hair must be stripped close as described in the text.

Diagram 19. The trimmed foot of the Silky Terrier as it should appear.

your palm covering the front of the handle, fingers curving around the back of the handle and thumb resting on the blade, as shown in the Equipment Chapter. Ruffle up a bit of hair between the blade and your thumb. Press your thumb firmly against the hair and blade and when working on the legs, pull the hair straight down in the direction that it grows. Do not strip with an upward motion; this cuts off all the hair and creates a choppy look. Remember to strip a small area at a time to shorten the feathering only and not make the leg look bare.

You should strip each back leg from the hock joint to the foot and each front leg from the first joint (or bend in the leg) to the foot. Do not remove any of the long leg feathering above these areas. When the stripping is finished, comb the long hair above the knees and hocks downward. It should not touch the ground.

Scissor the excess hair from between the pads underneath each foot. Then place the foot down in a normal standing position and scissor around each paw to remove any hairs that extend beyond the outline of the foot. Diagram 19 illustrates trimmed legs and feet.

TAIL: The Silky Terrier's tail should be well-coated but devoid of plume. The hair should be from 1 to 1-1/2 inches long, with feathering from 1 to 2 inches. The easiest way to trim the tail is to hold the tip with your free hand, and strip or use thinning shears to remove any excess feathering to make the tail look neat.

EARS: Comb the hair on the ears with the fine-tooth flea comb to remove as much dead hair as possible. The Silky's ears should be high-set, erect and have a sleek appearance. Any long or straggly hairs on the outside and inside of each ear and around the edges should be plucked on the dog to be shown in the breed ring. Plucking is removing dead hair with the thumb and index finger and is more comfortable than stripping for the sensitive areas on the dog's head and ears. The correct plucking technique is to grasp a few hairs firmly between your index finger and thumb, holding the hair near the skin and pulling backward with a slight twisting motion. The ears are usually the most difficult area to trim and, if you find plucking unsatisfactory, dust your fingers with silicone grooming powder or chalk for a better grip before you pull out the hairs.

On the pet Silky Terrier, you may clip the ears with a #10 or #15 blade and scissor around the edges to remove any straggly hairs.

BODY: Stand the dog on the grooming table. As in Yorkshire Terriers, use the edge of the comb to part the hair from the stop between the eyes, up over the skull and straight down the center of the back to the base of the tail. Comb the body hair on each side of the part straight down. When the part is straight, spray the back with a light mist of coat dressing, aerosol protein conditioner or the "dry type" hair spray made for men. Comb the hair on the front of the chest downward. The body coat should be from 5 to 6 inches long and does not touch the ground.

HEAD: Separate the hair at the front and back of each ear. The ears must always be erect. The topknot hair above the eyes should be combed to either side of the part. The Silky Terrier's dark eyes should always be seen and, if the topknot hair is too long and falls into the eyes, it should be plucked shorter. Do not scissor off any of the topknot hair; it will spoil the piercingly keen expression called for in the breed

Photograph 150. This beautiful headstudy can teach anyone a great deal about proper head trimming for the Silky Terrier. The ears are immaculately trimmed, the topknot is the right size and the keen, terrier expression is displayed to advantage.

Photograph 151. Although he is a Toy, the Silky Terrier should strongly display Terrier characteristics. His coat must be parted down the back and hang straight down, and while of sufficient length, it should not approach the coat length of a Yorkshire Terrier.

standard. Comb the hair on the muzzle backward and downward, in the direction of its growth. Long, unruly hairs around the eyes or muzzle which detract from the dog's expression may be plucked. To make unruly muzzle hair stay in place, spray a little coat oil on your fingers, then rub onto the hair and comb in place. Photograph 150 shows a close-up of the finished head.

Photograph 151 shows the finished Silky Terrier.

Suggestions for Coat Care

To be sure the ears stay erect on your show puppy, pluck the hair from the ears as soon as it starts growing long. This can be accomplished at about four months of age and will train your puppy to accept plucking.

For growing and maintaining the show coat, refer to the Yorkshire Terrier Chapter. Although the Silky Terrier's coat is shorter than that of the Yorkshire Terrier, the coat types are similar and instructions found in the Yorkshire Terrier Chapter would apply to both breeds.

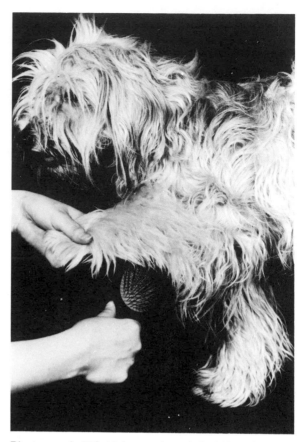

Photograph 152. Using a pin or bristle brush, brush the leg furnishings of the Tibetan Terrier toward the body, taking care not to tear our live hairs.

Photograph 153. The hair on the hindlegs is also brushed upward. When working on the legs, hold the foot in your hand. Holding the leg up by the hock, for example, will make the dog fidget unnecessarily.

The Tibetan Terrier

The Tibetan Terrier is a rare, medium-sized shaggy dog which has sometimes been described as an Old English Sheepdog in miniature. It is a distinct breed in its own right, however, which originated in Tibet hundreds of years ago. The Tibetan Terrier should be from 14 to 16 inches in height at the shoulder and weigh between 15 to thirty pounds. The body is compact and powerful and covered with a profuse coat. Forelegs and hind legs are heavily furnished. The feet are large, round and heavily furnished with hair between the toes and pads. The tail is well feathered and carried in a gay curl over the back. Eyes are large and dark. The Tibetan Terrier should have pendant, "V" shaped ears which are heavily feathered. The head should be well furnished with long hair falling forward over the eyes. The lower jaw has a small but not over-exaggerated amount of beard. This breed has a double coat. The undercoat is like fine wool and the top coat profuse and fine, but not silky or wooly. It should be long and either straight or waved.

The Tibetan Terrier needs no clipping or stripping. This is one of the few breeds where pets and show dogs should be groomed to look natural. Regular coat care is a must and there are a few additional steps necessary to make the Tibetan look natural but neat.

Brushing and Combing

Use a slicker brush on a puppy or dog with a badly matted coat. A pin or natural bristle brush is recommended for the show coat. Before brushing, spray the hair with an aerosol protein conditioner or coat dressing to minimize hair breakage. Brush the front legs upward from the feet to the chest, as shown in Photograph 152. Brush the back legs upward from the feet towards the tail, as shown in Photograph 153. Brush the tail towards the body. The long body hair should be brushed in the layering method described in the Brushing Chapter. The fall over the eyes should be brushed upward and backward and the beard should be brushed downward, as shown in Photograph 154. When the dog is completely brushed, stand him on the grooming table and brush the long hair to either side, as shown in Photograph 155.

The correct comb for the Tibetan Terrier is the Twinco #90 comb with long teeth with rounded ends to prevent scratching and skin irritation, described in the

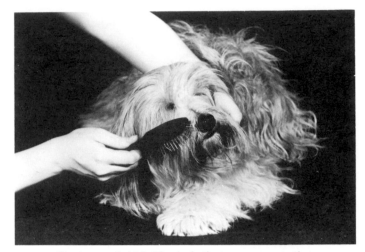

Photograph 154. The hair that grows over the eyes should be brushed back toward the neck. The beard is brushed down on either side of the muzzle.

Photograph 155. After having completely brushed out the coat, use the pin brush to lay the coat down on the sides.

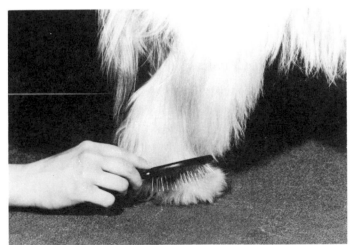

Photograph 156. Use a pin brush to fan out the hair on the feet. Any untidy wisps can be scissored off, but take care not to give an overtrimmed look to the feet.

Equipment Chapter. Comb through the entire coat to be sure all mats and tangles are removed.

Pre-Bath Preparations or Once Every Month

Clean ears, cut nails and check anal glands.

Bathing and Drying

Follow instructions in the Bathing Chapter for bathing and drying the long, flowing coated breeds. Shampoo twice and rinse well. A creme rinse is not usually suggested for show coats as it softens the coat too much. However, on pets and puppies, a creme rinse is recommended as it helps to make the hair more manageable between groomings.

Finishing the Tibetan Terrier

FEET: Fan out the feet furnishings with the pin brush, as shown in Photograph 156. The Standard calls for large, round, heavily feathered feet. If any straggly hairs detract from the round appearance, they may be removed with scissors, but it should not be obvious that any scissoring has been done. Do not remove the hair from between the pads underneath the feet.

Photograph 157. Use a knitting needle or the end tooth of a comb to make a straight part from the top of the skull to the base of the tail.

Photograph 158. Here is the fully groomed body coat of the Tibetan Terrier with the center part properly fashioned.

Photograph 159. This type of presentation is often preferred among pet owners. Here the dog is groomed without the part.

BODY AND LEGS: Stand the dog on the grooming table with hindquarters facing you. Using the edge of a comb or a knitting needle, part the hair from the top of the skull straight down the back to the tail, as shown in Photograph 157. When the coat has been parted, brush the long hair to either side and down the legs. The finished body is shown in Photograph 158. There is another shaggy look for the Tibetan Terrier shown in Photograph 159. This style is more popular with pet owners, since it is difficult to keep the straight center part looking presentable most of the time. Either look, with or without the part, is correct.

THE HEAD: Photograph 160 shows the Tibetan's head before finishing. Brush the fall forward; brush the moustache out and downward, and brush the beard downward. The hair may be parted to divide the coat evenly on both sides, as shown in Photograph 161. The hair over the eyes should be allowed to fall naturally and must never be pulled back. Photograph 162 shows the finished head.

Photograph 163 shows the finished Tibetan Terrier.

Coat Care

The Tibetan Terrier should be brushed two to three times a week. When a puppy is about a year old, he may seem to be shedding excessively while the coat becomes coarser. This means that the puppy coat is changing into adult texture. After this change-over period, you will find shedding minimal.

Refer to the Chapter on Lhasa Apsos for additional coat care suggestions.

Photograph 160. The ungroomed head of a Tibetan Terrier.

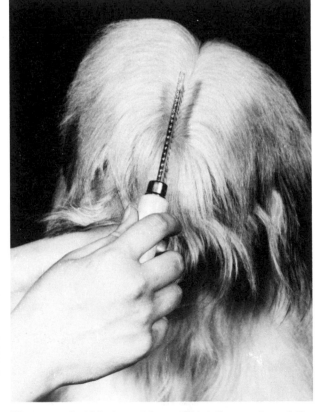

Photograph 161. A part is made at the center of the skull and the hair is combed evenly to either side.

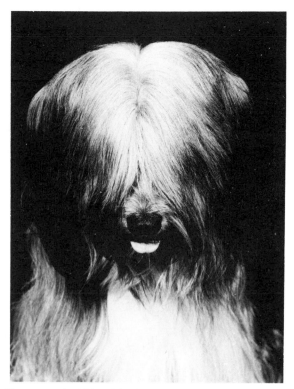

Photograph 162. This is what the Tibetan Terrier head should look like after grooming. It should be noted that the eyes in this breed are always covered by the fall.

Photograph 163. This shows the Tibetan Terrier fully groomed, head and body. Some have likened the breed to a miniature Old English Sheepdog, but the Tibetan is a distinct breed full of a charm and appeal of its own.

Photograph 164. The Toy Manchester Terrier is the smaller and younger variety of this old breed. His coat is easy to keep clean and in order, requiring but light trimming in preparation for a show or any other special occasion. *Brown.*

The Toy Manchester Terrier

Description of Coat

The Breed Standard describes the coat as "Smooth, short, thick, dense, close and glossy; not soft." The Toy Manchester Terrier's color is jet black and rich mahogany tan.

Care of the Pet Dog

The Toy Manchester Terrier requires a minimum of difficult grooming. As is the case with all short-haired breeds, the most important factor comes from within. Feeding your dog properly, plus regular conditioning, is the basis for a healthy, shining coat. The easiest way to keep the coat in good condition is to brush regularly with a fine-quality bristle brush. Use medium-soft bristles that will not scratch the dog, but will get into the skin to remove the dead hair and dirt. Follow directions for "Short Haired Dogs" in the Brushing Chapter.

Once a month, pet Toy Manchester Terriers should have nails trimmed, ears cleaned, teeth and anal glands checked and whiskers trimmed. A short-haired dog seldom needs a bath if groomed regularly. An occasional rubdown with a sponge or terry towel moistened with a Dri-Bath shampoo or coat dressing will keep the coat lustrous and clean. When bathing is necessary, follow instructions found in the Bathing Chapter.

Care of the Show Dog

If you intend to show your Toy Manchester Terrier, there are a few additional steps to follow to prepare the dog for the ring. This additional grooming will take only a few minutes a day or two before the show. The Toy Manchester Terrier should have a sleek, sculptured outline and there may be some thinning necessary to remove untidy hairs that stick out to spoil the sleek look. *Remember, you only want to thin a few straggly hairs; you must not overtrim and make bare spots!* Please turn to the show grooming suggestions for the Miniature Pinscher and follow instructions for the finishing touches for the show ring.

Photograph 164 shows the finished Toy Manchester Terrier.

Photograph 165. This Yorkshire Terrier is in the glorious bloom of a full show coat. While there is hardly anything in dogs that can match it for beauty, the care of such a coat represents many hours of careful and skillful grooming.

Photograph 166. The coat of this pet Yorkshire shows the effects of total neglect. Compare this coat to the coat on the show dog.

Photograph 167. Here is a front view of the same pet before grooming. Regular attention would have been easy, pleasant and sufficient to forestall this dog's condition and the measures necessary to correct it.

The Yorkshire Terrier

Description of Coat

The breed standard describes the ideal coat texture and color as:

"Coat—Quality, texture and quantity of coat are of prime importance. Hair is glossy, fine and silky in texture. Coat on the body is moderately long and perfectly straight (not wavy). It may be trimmed to floor length to give ease of movement and a neater appearance, if desired. The fall on the head is long, tied with one bow in center of head or parted in the middle and tied with two bows. Hair on the muzzle is very long. Hair should be trimmed short on tips of ears and may be trimmed on feet to give them a neat appearance."

"Colors—Puppies are born black and tan and are normally darker in body color, showing an intermingling of black hair in the tan until they are matured. Color of hair on body and richness of tan on head and legs are of prime importance in ADULT DOGS to which the following color requirements apply:

  Blue—Is a dark steel blue, not a silver blue and not mingled with fawn, bronzy or black hairs.

  Tan—All tan hair is darker at the roots than in the middle, shading to still lighter tan at the tips. There should be no sooty or black hair intermingled with any of the tan."

"Color On Body—The blue extends over the body from back of neck, to root of tail. Hair on tail is a darker blue, especially at end of tail.

  Headfall—A rich golden tan, deeper in color at sides of head, at ear roots and on the muzzle, with ears a deep rich tan. Tan color should not extend down on back of neck.

  Chest and Legs—A bright rich tan, not extending above the elbow on the forelegs nor above the stifle on the hind legs."

Grooming Instructions

The Yorkshire Terrier shown in Photograph 165 is in show coat. Photograph 166 shows a side view, and Photograph 167, a front view of a neglected pet Yorkshire Terrier. Basically, the grooming procedure is the same and the pet will be used to illustrate most of this chapter. Special pointers for caring for the show coat are included at the end of these grooming instructions.

Brushing and Combing

The correct brush for the Yorkshire Terrier is a natural bristle brush. There are certain types of coats on which you can use a pin brush, but the bristle brush is usually the best choice. On matted pets, you may need to use the small size slicker brush. The correct comb is the half-fine and half-medium style illustrated in the Equipment Chapter. You will also need an extra-fine tooth flea comb for the beard.

The close-up of the head area of the pet indicates that there is an accumulation of food and dirt caked in the whiskers and that the fall is matted from hanging into the eyes. To prevent loss of hair when grooming such a matted dog, rub a liquid tangle remover into the matted areas to loosen the dirt while you brush the body first.

Brush the hair under the chest as instructed for long, flowing coated breeds in the Brushing Chapter. Brush the long body coat as directed in the Brushing Chapter.

Brushing the Head

Sit the dog on the grooming table while you brush the head. Brush the hair on top of the head away from the eyes, as shown in Photograph 168. Brush the hair on the sides of the head and muzzle, taking care not to injure the eyes with the bristles or pins on the brush. Photograph 169 shows the use of the extra-fine-tooth flea comb with handle to remove matter near the eye corners. Photograph 170 shows the use of the

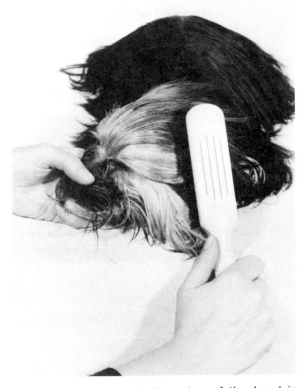

Photograph 168. The hair on top of the head is brushed away from the eyes, using a bristle or pin brush.

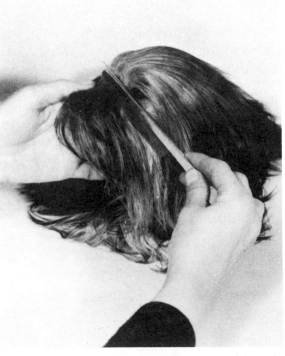

Photograph 169. Like many other coated breeds, the Yorkshire Terrier will accumulate matter in the eye corners. This should be gently removed with a fine-toothed flea comb.

Photograph 170. Food particles that accumulate in the whiskers are removed with the flea comb. Using a liquid detangler first makes these particles come out easier and with less discomfort for the dog.

Photograph 171. Stand the male dog on his hind legs and clip around the genital area. This will keep him much neater.

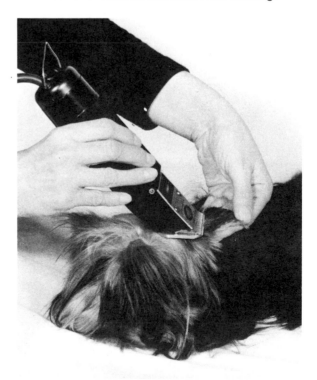

Photograph 172. This pet Yorkshire's ears are being trimmed with clippers. Scissors, thinning shears and the finger and thumb method have also been used.

comb removing food particles in the whiskers. If you soaked these areas in a tangle remover before brushing, the foreign matter should be easy to remove.

Combing

After the hair has been thoroughly brushed, comb through the hair, using the medium end of the comb, to be sure all tangles are removed.

Pre-Bath Preparations

Clean ears, cut toenails and check anal glands.

Bathing and Drying

Before putting the dog in the water, part the hair down the center of the back. Follow instructions found in the Bathing Chapter. Give two shampoos and wash the head area with a tearless shampoo. If the whiskers and hair under the eyes are badly stained, dip a toothbrush into the shampoo and gently scrub these areas. Use a creme rinse. Always brush the coat dry. While the dryer blows on the wet hair, keep the part in the center of the back as you brush each side downward in the direction that it grows.

Finishing the Yorkshire Terrier

STOMACH: Use a #10 or #15 blade to clip the hair from the genitals of the male Yorkshire Terrier, as shown in Photograph 171.

EARS: The upper part of the ears should be clipped. Using a #15 blade on pets and a #40 on show dogs, clip both sides of the top 2/3rds of each ear, as shown in Photograph 172. Then scissor around the edges of each ear, as shown in Photograph 173, to remove any straggly hairs and emphasize the point at the top.

FEET: Scissor the excess hair from between the pads underneath each foot, as shown

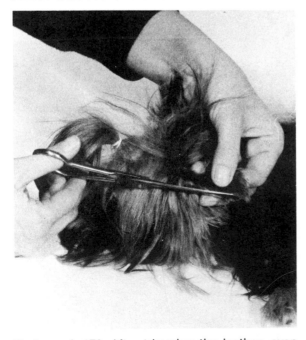

Photograph 173. After trimming the leather, even edge of the ear with scissors taking care to emphasize the point.

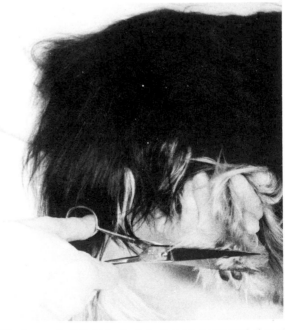

Photograph 174. Trim hair between pads and shape foot to roundness as required in the breed standard.

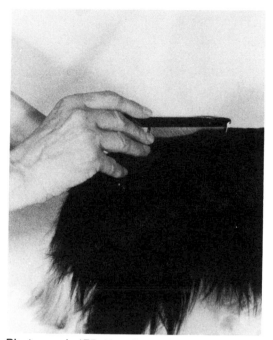

Photograph 175. Use the end of a comb or a knitting needle to make a straight part down the back from the base of the skull to the set-on of the tail.

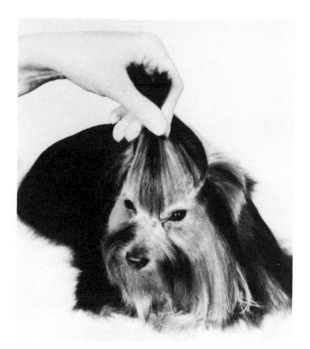

Photograph 176. Begin the topknot by parting the hair from the outside corner of each eye to the inside corner of each ear.

in Photograph 174. Then place the foot down in a normal standing position. Holding up any long leg hair with your free hand, comb the hair on the foot, fanning the coat out in a circle. Scissor around each foot, shaping it into a large circle.

BODY: Stand the dog on the grooming table. Use the edge of the comb, as shown in Photograph 175, to part the hair from the top of the nose up over the skull and straight down the center of the back to the tail. Comb the body hair on each side of the part straight down. When the part is straight, spray the back with a light mist of coat dressing, aerosol protein conditioner or the "dry type" hair spray made for men. Comb the hair on the front of the chest downward.

HEAD: Using the edge of the comb, part the hair on the head from the outside corner of each eye upward to the inside corner of each ear, as shown in Photograph 176. Next, part the hair straight across the top of the head from the inside corner of one ear to the inside corner of the other ear, as shown in Photograph 177. Twist a small latex band around this hair to hold the forelocks, as shown in Photograph 178. The rest of the hair may be braided, as shown in Photograph 179, or left long and doubled over with the latex band twisted once again to hold the hair in place, as shown in Photograph 180. You may use a small bow or piece of bright colored yarn to complete the finishing touches.

Photograph 181 shows the finished Yorkshire Terrier pet and Photograph 182 shows the finished show Yorkshire Terrier.

Suggestions for Coat Care

To be sure the ears stay erect on your show puppy, clip the hair on the inside and outside of the top 2/3rds of each ear, as soon as the hair starts growing long. This can be started at three to four months of age.

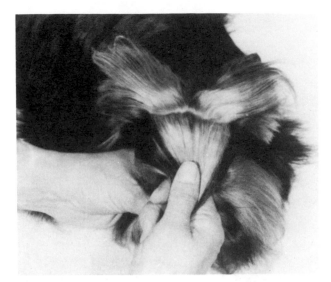

Photograph 177. The next step in fashioning the top-knot is making a parting across the top of the dog's head from ear to ear.

Photograph 178. Use a small latex band to hold the forelock in place. A bright-colored bow attached to the band enhances the picture.

Photograph 179. Some owners prefer the top-knot braided above the bow as shown here.

Photograph 180. Another style of putting up the topknot is to double over the long hair and twist the latex around it.

Photograph 181. Here is the same pet Yorkshire that was shown at the beginning of this chapter, and the difference is graphic! This little dog may never win a ribbon, but groomed and well-presented he displays all the charm of his kind.

Photograph 182. To develop a coat like this a Yorkshire must come from a family of good coats and the owner must be prepared to devote the necessary time to the dog's condition. There can be no short-cuts to the show preparation of this breed.

Growing and maintaining a show coat can be difficult for a novice. A puppy should be brushed two to three times a week. Always use a coat conditioner or coat dressing before you brush the hair to reduce static electricity and coat breakage. While the puppy is young, get him accustomed to having the hard-to-get spots brushed and combed—under the chest, under the front and back legs and on the beard. The puppy should be bathed every 10 days to two weeks. Eyes need attention every day. If you own a male Yorkie and have a problem with stained or matted feathering under the body from urine residue, sponge off the stomach every other day in between regular shampoos.

As the Yorkie's coat starts growing longer, keep the hair oiled in between shows to encourage growth and prevent it from breaking off. Because coat textures differ, you will have to experiment a bit to find out which is the right product to use. Certain textures gum up with the use of one product and respond beautifully to another. To keep the hair oiled, use a light oil in aerosol form, such as Ring 5, Pro-Groom or St. Aubrey Coatasheen. You may wish to use a slightly heavier oil such as Ring 5 Bright & Shine, St. Aubrey Royal Coatalin, Alpha Keri or Lubath (these last two are purchased in a drug store). The Royal Coatalin comes in paraffin form and can be brushed into the coat by running the pin brush through the Coatalin block, then through the coat. Royal Coatalin can also be melted in a pie pan on top of the stove and brushed into the hair in liquid form. The Lubath can be poured directly from the bottle onto the coat and brushed through the hair. The Alpha Keri is best applied after the dog has been bathed and rinsed. While the Yorkie is still wet, just before you remove him from the tub, pour the following mixture over the coat. Mix one capful of Alpha Keri with four cups of warm water (you may also add your creme rinse to this mixture) and stir the mixture enough for the oil and water to blend. Pour the Alpha Keri mixture over the coat and squeeze the mixture through the hair to be sure all areas are covered. Rinse lightly, take the dog out of the tub and dry as usual. This will make the Yorkie's coat glisten. Remember, however, that when you show your Yorkshire Terrier, he should be bathed the day before the show and *no oil of any type rinsed into the coat.* Only a creme rinse should be used the day before the show.

Do not over-oil the hair. This only clogs the pores and slows down hair growth. When keeping the show dog in any coat preparation, it's best to bathe every 10 days to two weeks to prevent excessive dirt build-up caused by the oil on the hair.

As soon as the hair above the eyes is long enough it should be wrapped to encourage growth and prevent breakage. In between shows, the long body coat may also be wrapped to protect the ends of the coat and prevent damage. Instructions and photographs are found in "Wrapping The Show Coat."